Praise for iN aLL tHinGs

"These teenage voices are clear, genuine, and grace-filled. Anyone who doubts the profound spiritual hunger of adolescents and the necessity of teaching them to pray should read this book."

—JULIE A. COLLINS, spiritual director
Jesuit Center for Spiritual Growth, Wernersville, Pennsylvania

"These prayers by young men and women from Jesuit high schools are privileged expressions of praying as searching, finding, and being challenged by God. As such, they are a witness to grace and a sign of hope."

—HOWARD GRAY, S.J., rector of the Jesuit community
John Carroll University

"These are great prayers! . . . I highly recommend this book for high school students, for their parents, their teachers, and the broader group of faith-filled persons and searchers. It can help for personal prayer, for prayer moving beyond formulas, and for genuine friendship with God. Take the book and sit with it, reading just a prayer or two at a time, but slowly. Then make the prayer your own."

—JAMES STOEGER, S.J., provincial assistant for secondary education
Chicago Province of the Society of Jesus

More praise for iN aLL tHinGs

"A book of prayers not only for students, but for parents. There could be no better way to understand teenagers than through their prayers. These prayers are revealing and hope-filled reflections on the youth of today."

—ROSEMARY CROGHAN, chairwoman of the board
Cristo Rey Jesuit High School

"*In All Things,* a compilation of familiar prayer accompanied by messages from students to God, is an inspiring testament to the power of faith and the wisdom of young people."

—JOSEPH CALIFANO, president, The National Center
on Addiction and Substance Abuse, Columbia University

"*In All Things* reveals the holy longings of teenagers to discern God's presence in their lives and in their worlds. Meditating on their prayers and hearing the Spirit moving young hearts is spiritually invigorating. Congratulations to Mike Daley, Lee Yeazell, and the contributing students for bringing us a contemporary prayer book by and for our young people (and for us older folk as well!). I incorporated Andy Novak's "Peace Is . . ." into a Eucharistic Liturgy as a post-communion reflection. It worked very nicely."

—JOSEPH F. O'CONNELL, S.J, president, JSEA

iN aLL tHinGs

iN aLL tHinGs

Everyday Prayers of
Jesuit High School Students

EDITED BY MICHAEL J. DALEY
AND LEE P. YEAZELL

LOYOLA PRESS.
A JESUIT MINISTRY

Chicago

LOYOLAPRESS.
A JESUIT MINISTRY

3441 N. Ashland Avenue
Chicago, Illinois 60657
(800) 621-1008
www.loyolapress.com

Cover and interior design by Megan Duffy Rostan
Cover photo by Noeru Takizawa/Photonica

Library of Congress Cataloging-in-Publication Data

In all things : everyday prayers of Jesuit high school students / edited
by Michael J. Daley and Lee P. Yeazell.
    p. cm.
  ISBN-13: 978-0-8294-1957-3
  ISBN-10: 0-8294-1957-8
 1. Catholic high school students--Prayer-books and devotions--
English.
2. Jesuits--Prayer-books and devotions--English. I. Daley, Michael J.,
1968- II. Yeazell, Lee P.
  BX2150 .I55 2003
  242'.802--dc21

                                                2002152125

Printed in the United States of America
            11 12 Versa 10 9 8 7

To Jesuit students past, present, and future

CoNtEnTs

FoReWorD

A popular bumper sticker reads: "You are a child of God. Please call home."

"Calling home" is what the young people in this book are doing. Their "calls" echo the same four themes that we find in the prayers of Jesus and his disciples. They are petition, contrition, thanksgiving, and praise.

1. PETITION

Jesus prays, "Father, for you all things are possible; remove this cup from me." (Mark 14:36) An anonymous student calls to God for help in "A Prayer for Separated Parents":

> Dear Lord, help me face the daily challenge of having separated parents. Help me.
>
> Give me the strength to overcome the difficulties I have in planning visits and help me face the tough decisions I must make.
>
> When my parents argue, ease the rage and confusion I feel.

I also pray that you help my parents through their hard times, and that one day they will become friends.

2. CONTRITION

A tax collector prays with downcast eyes in the temple, "God, be merciful to me, a sinner!" (Luke 18:13) Young Matt prays with a similar repentant heart in "How Many Times":

> How many times have I stood in awe before the beauty of your creation and then turned around and defaced it?
>
> How many times have I seen your immense love for me, and how many times have I rejected that love?
>
> As many times as you have forgiven me in your infinite compassion.

3. THANKSGIVING

Jesus prays, "I thank you, Father, Lord of heaven and earth, because you have hidden these things from the wise and the intelligent and have revealed them to infants." (Luke 10:21) Young Anthony prays to the Father in a similar spirit of gratitude in "The Rock":

> You have brought me to this place,
>   this school.
> I entered it a mere boy, childish and immature,
>   but I shall leave a "man for others,"
>   ready . . . to "set the world on fire," . . .
>
> Every step of the way, I thank you, God, not only through this prayer,

but in every essay I write,
in every test I take,
and every ball I shoot.

4. PRAISE

Thomas the Apostle fell on his knees before Jesus and prayed, "My Lord and my God!" (John 20:28) The poetic heart of Julie echoes a similar awe in the presence of her Lord and God in "Spring":

In the sweet fluttering of apple blossoms you cascade around me,

> Dancing in front of my eyes . . .
> Soaring like butterflies . . .

> So that when I go home
> Hours later,
> I find white snowdrop petals
> Nestling in my clothes.

Don Sibert once said, "What comes from the heart touches the heart." That is what makes the prayers of these young people ring true. They come from the heart.

*   *   *   *   *

That brings us to how to use the prayers in this book.

1. **Select the prayer on which you have chosen to meditate.** For example, take "The Pressure Prayer" composed by Jim:

   Lord, why are there all these pressures in the world?
   Pressure to be cool,
           To be popular,
           To be athletic,
           To be smart.
   How can I be myself?

2. **Set the stage for your meditation by praying the following:**

   Father, you created me
   and put me on earth for a purpose.

   Jesus, you died for me
   and called me to complete your work.

   Holy Spirit, you help me
   to carry out the work
   for which I was created and called.
   In your presence and name—
   Father, Son, and Spirit—
   I begin my meditation.

   May all my thoughts and inspirations
   have their origin in you
   and be directed to your glory.

3. **Read the student prayer you have chosen slowly and prayerfully.**

   When you finish reading it, return to any phrase, sentence, or idea that struck you.

   Think about the phrase, sentence, or idea that struck you. Why do you think it struck you?

   Listen to God's response. What may God be saying to you personally through it?

4. **End your meditation by doing two things:**

   a. Jot down in your "prayer journal" something from your meditation that you would be willing to share with others; and

   b. Compose a prayer based on your meditation that you would be willing to share with others.

*   *   *   *   *

There is one final point that anyone beginning a prayer journey should keep in mind, especially about the "prayer of petition."

Years ago, a man lived in a rural area where clothing stores carried only the essential items, like socks and underwear. He bought all other clothing from a mail-order house. On each order form was this question:

> If we don't have in stock the article you ordered, may we send a substitute similar to the one you ordered?

On one of his orders, the man wrote "yes."

A week later, he was thrilled to death when the mail-order house sent him a beautiful substitute listed at twice the price, but at no extra cost. From that point on, the man always printed "yes" after that question. He even hoped they didn't have the item in stock, so they'd send him something better.

The man compared the mail-order form to our prayer requests to God. He wrote:

> When we pray, we should never omit telling God we'll gladly accept a substitute, because when God substitutes something, it's always far better than what we asked for.

This is the important point of a familiar poem found in the pocket of a dead Confederate soldier. It reads:

> I asked God for strength, that I might achieve;
> I was made weak, that I might learn humbly to obey.
> I asked for health, that I might do greater things;
> I was given infirmity, that I might do better things.
> I asked for riches, that I might be happy;
> I was given poverty, that I might be wiser.
> I asked for power, that I might have the praise of men;
> I was given weakness, that I might feel the need of God.
> I asked for all things, that I might enjoy life;
> I was given life, that I might enjoy all things.
> I got nothing that I asked for
> —but everything I had hoped for.
> Almost despite myself,
> my unspoken prayers were answered.
> I am, among all men, most richly blessed.

MARK LINK, S.J.

PREFACE

It's a desire that springs from the heart of the Gospels. We yearn for a closer relationship with Jesus Christ and with each other; we cry out, "We want to talk with you God, yet we're at a loss. We don't know how. Help us, Lord, teach us how to pray."

Whether that prayerful relationship is in the form of petition, adoration, contrition, or thanksgiving (PACT), prayer opens us up to God, others, and ourselves. In the process, we become more like the one to whom we are praying—the loving Father, the faithful Son, the enlivening Spirit.

Aware of the importance of prayer, Rev. Jim Stoeger, S.J., approached us about a project that he wished to see become a reality: a book of prayers devoted to the Ignatian ideal of "finding God in all things." The book he envisioned came not from the classroom, but from the lived experience of high school youth. We quickly took him up on his invitation and began soliciting all the Jesuit high schools in the United States. In the letters sent out to educators, we asked that they send in prayers by students that spoke of finding God and faith in a myriad of ways—the challenge of a mission trip, the confusion of belief, the joy of loved ones, the grief of death, the anxiety of adolescence—the possibilities were endless.

The depth, sincerity, and emotion of the submitted prayers overwhelmed us. You name the theme, they touched upon it. We also found that our own thoughts, concerns, and prayers were voiced and shared by these students. And now we encourage you—whether student, teacher, administrator, or parent—to discover yourself in these prayers.

Young adults are starving for meaningful, prayerful material that is relevant and speaks to their experience. These prayers do just that. Youth ministers and catechists can use the prayers in this collection to serve as introduction or closing to a particular faith topic. Or particular prayers can be used to set up an issue that will be addressed on a retreat or discussed in a class or meeting. Parents will be reassured that though their son or daughter may not express it at home, they feel and are able to articulate spiritual hunger.

Finally, we would like to express our gratitude: First of all to the students who submitted prayers and participated in the project, though we were not able to include all of them, thank you. We could not have done it without you. This book is what it is because of you. To the educators who gave their students the opportunity to take part, we say thank you as well. Know that your cooperation was appreciated. We hope that we were not too much of a nuisance! To our fellow colleagues and administrators at St. Xavier High School, the staff at Loyola Press, and to Fr. Mark Link, S.J., thank you for your support and encouragement. Finally, to our own families, thank you for being there and giving us the time to make this possible.

Prayers for the Journey: Students' Prayers

The Rock

Dear God,
You have brought me to this place,
    this school.
I entered it a mere boy, childish and immature,
    but I shall leave a "man for others,"
    ready to take on the world.
Each day I work harder to accomplish that,
  to "set the world on fire,"
    to let others know not only who I am,
    but who you are.
It is a place you have called me to be,
    a place where you have bestowed upon me
    an opportunity of infinite possibilities
    and immense proportions.
Every time I open my locker,
    every time I walk into class,
    I am grateful for what you have given to me.
Every step of the way, I thank you, God, not only
  through this prayer,
    but in every essay I write,
    in every test I take,
    and every ball I shoot.
Thank God for my school.
Amen.

ANTHONY DAYRIT
Rockhurst High School
Kansas City, Missouri

E-PRAYER

To: God@I'mtheboss.com
From: me@students.com
Re: when was the last time?

Dear God:
How long has it been since I spoke to you? So much time
has passed. I have been really busy, and I know that's not
an excuse; I'm pretty sure my teachers would agree. I think
it's been a while, geez . . . Remember the last time?
Wow, you really pulled me through, just when I was going
to give up and lie down, you saved me. I don't think I'll
ever forget that without you I wouldn't be where I am
today; that without you, I'd be nothing. So I write to you
now to thank you for being there for me, even though I've
almost never been there for you.
Thanks a lot.

Sincerely,

Me

P.S. E-mail me sometime.

MARIO CERVANTES
Strake Jesuit College Preparatory
Houston, Texas

ALONe

A girl,
Her cheeks flushed
From cold,
Wild hair flung
In the wind,
Lost
On a cold, dark street,
ALONE
She begs to be helped,
For her prayers to be answered.
I dislike her,
But no,
Not her,
The people who did not help her,
And that would include
Me.
But I am afraid.
Afraid to be cold, lost, and
ALONE
Please,
Give me strength.
Amen.

ALLISON NAVIA
Cheverus High School
Portland, Maine

SoMeTiMeS

Sometimes, God, sometimes I think
  I'm on top of everything.
Nothing can stop me, and I have everything worked out
  for myself, for once.
Sometimes, God, sometimes I think quietly to myself,
How can it possibly get any worse than this?
What am I supposed to do? How can everything be so wrong?
Sometimes, God, sometimes I wonder how it is
  no matter how hard I try,
I'll never understand why it didn't happen differently.
Sometimes, God, sometimes I wonder what my future
  will be like
and if it will have as many ups and downs, twists and
  turns, that the road to my past has.
No matter what I go through, God, there is one thing
  I know for certain:
You will be there with me through it all,
        Every time.

CHRIS SIROLLI
St. Joseph's Preparatory School
Philadelphia, Pennsylvania

PRAYER FOR A JESUIT FRESHMAN

God, please help me through this
perilous journey called high school.
It is going to be tough.
I'll need your help and guidance
to make it through successfully.
I will face many decisions that will affect the rest of my life
and probably shape who I will be in the future.
Give me the courage to strive for the *magis* in all I do.
Help me with my schoolwork and
with my sports careers and other extracurriculars.
Help me with my relationships with others
and to control myself and my actions.
Help me to help myself and others less fortunate than me
and to manage time for work
and time for play.
Help me to remember to spend time with my friends
and time with my family.
Help me so that when I make mistakes,
I may learn from them.
Help me to do my best in all I do

and to help others to succeed too.
Help me to deal with the issues surrounding me,
with my family and friends,
my city and my country.
Help me to be more like Jesus,
to see God in all things,
so that I will be able to deal with the disappointments
that I may face,
and be grateful and humble when the rewards come my way.
Take me under your wing,
and protect me from physical and emotional damage,
yet also let me be myself and try new things.
Lord, let your love and consideration
shine upon my peers and me.
And most of all, help me to become "a person for others."
Amen.

DAN SHEA
St. Xavier High School
Cincinnati, Ohio

OH GOD, PLEASE

Please help me on my long and tiring journey through life:
. . . be my legs when I cannot walk,
. . . be my eyes when I need to see the beauty in all things,
. . . be my ears when I need to hear the call of others,
. . . be my mouth when I need to comfort others,
. . . be my arms when I need to embrace others.
Please find me and take me back when I am lost.
Please continue to help me do my best in everything I do,
   standing by me every step of the way,
   as you always have done.
Help me to be proud of all that I do and stand with me
   when I feel that I am alone, for when we work together
   we are an unbeatable team . . . able to accomplish anything.
Please help me to live every day to its fullest,
   as well as enjoy life for all that it is worth.
I love you, God, and will honor every second of life simply
   because it is a gift from you, oh Lord.
      Amen.

BRIAN LANG
Saint Peter's Preparatory School
Jersey City, New Jersey

HIS CREATION

Lord, you are almighty and powerful.
You breathed life into all of us;
with your omnipotent hand you molded the world.
Michelangelo painted the Sistine Chapel
the way you painted the skies,
and he sculpted the exquisite *David,*
but you carved the lands and seas.
You made a heaven above the heavens
and gave your children the power to get there.
Even after our world, you were still at work
making other worlds for us
to explore.
You made the brightest lights nature has ever seen,
such as the light that shined so brightly
at the birth of your son,
Christ.
And still you work,
with every flower that blooms,
every child that is born,
every source of life in all your creation,
you paint every moment on the canvas of life.

WALTER CURTIS
Fordham Preparatory School
Bronx, New York

Romans, Chapter 12

Keep it real.
Don't like bad things.
Hold tightly to the good things in life.
Love each other equally.
Be kind to one another and show respect to all.
Never lack enthusiasm.
Be a passionate soul.
Worship God and be dedicated to your love for him.
Be happy with future possibilities.
Wait out the bad times.
In order to keep going and not give up,
    you must turn to God for help.
Act as saints.
Be nice and loving even toward those who are cruel.
Chill with the chillers.
Be sincere with those who are suffering.
Be wise; harmonize.
Don't be proud, but spend time
    with the poor and unfortunate.

Don't act like you are better than you are.
Don't hate the haters.
Take good away from everything you experience.
Don't get even.
Treat your enemy like your friend.
Love the "hell" out of people.
Do not accept evil as okay or normal,
   but instead turn around the evil by doing good.

PAIGE ADEJARE, JENNY BRANDEMAIER,
PAT BURKE, GREG DOWDEN,
KIM DOYLE, J. J. GIBSON, MIKE GREEN,
BILL HANLEY, ELIZABETH HUSER,
EDDIE JOURNEY, ASHLEY KINKER,
MIKE KIRSH, REBECCA LOVEJOY,
ALEX MARCINIAK, GINNY MEZA,
ELIZABETH MOREAU, JACQUELINE NATZ,
BRIAN SCHNEIDER, KATIE SCHWENK, MATT
TRECO, HERMAN WHITFIELD
Brebeuf Jesuit College Preparatory School
Indianapolis, Indiana

Prayer for Light

God, turn me into a star
To shine in the darkness of the world.
My quiet light will defy the powers of hell
And become a beacon to guide all peoples back to you.
Amen.

EPHRAIM SASIS
University of Detroit Jesuit
  High School and Academy
Detroit, Michigan

CAn You HEaR ME?

Almighty and powerful God of the sky,
Why is it that you don't hear me cry?
Is it perhaps not loud enough to hear,
Or could it be that you don't really care?
What should I do, who should I be,
Why do you refuse to answer me?
I ask this aloud, now please answer my question,
For now all I can do is listen, listen, listen, listen.

Ah yes, now I see all that you are,
You're a God that can hear from near to far.
Not like any being that I can liken you to,
But a spirit, a force, not even a "you."
For "you" indicates a human connection,
But God is beyond my comprehension.
God's much more than you or I can imagine,
God is in all of us, a being to believe in.

So why is it that God still won't talk to me?
I'll ask what I'm supposed to do, but I still can't see.
Or maybe God tells me just what to do,
And I'm not listening; the response doesn't get through.
When will I see what God tells me?
In a week, or two, or maybe three?
I hope that soon I can open up and hear
The plan that God is trying to share.

GREG STEGEMAN
Loyola Academy
Wilmette, Illinois

A TeeNaGeR's PRaYeR oF CoNtRitIoN

Jesus, I come to you today praying for forgiveness.
I am sorry for the times when I judged people
Before even knowing who they are on the inside.
I'm sorry for the times when I gossiped,
Disregarding others' feelings to make myself feel better.
And, Jesus, I'm very sorry for the times today
When I took advantage of my family.
They are so good to me and deserve
    my love, respect, and appreciation.
Please forgive me, Jesus, for my sins and help me to show others
God's merciful love through my words and actions.
In Jesus' name I pray.
Amen.

JENNIFER KOMOS
Walsh Jesuit High School
Cuyahoga Falls, Ohio

SACRamENTaL AWaReNeSS

Dear God,

You made me a part of your family in baptism
  like Jesus was by John the Baptist, and I am thankful.
I received the Bread of Life during communion
  as an evil heart receives love for the first time.
My sins were forgiven on the day of penance,
  and I was thankful.
I received a religious name on confirmation,
  and my soul was fulfilled.
Later in my life I will meet a girl with whom
  I will celebrate the sacrament of holy matrimony.
  For this I will be thankful.
If God calls me for his special service, I will participate
  in holy orders and for this I will be thankful.
As I grow old, I will become weak and weary. My family
  will bring someone to help me in my final sacrament of
  anointing of the sick. When this is complete, my soul
  will be happy and I will be thankful.
Through all of these sacraments that I will complete,
  I hope that you will guide me, and when you do,
  I will be thankful. Amen.

NELSON GONZALEZ
St. Peter's Preparatory School
Jersey City, New Jersey

I Am There

I am there in all that you do—
In the predawn alarm and in the breakfast
    that gets you going.
On your trip to school, I am watching over you.
I hear your prayers in morning convocation.
Throughout the day I am listening, guiding, and teaching.
When you turn a deaf ear to gossip, I am there.
When you give to a friend in need, I am there.
In your time of need, I am there.

My strength is yours in the pregame meal.
I talk to you as you focus on your task.
I support you always because I am there.
In the cool night air as the·Stars and Stripes sways,
    I am there.
As you take the field and the crowd reaches fever pitch,
    I am there.
On every block, run, pass, and tackle, I am there.
As you strive to be the best you can be, I am there.
In your moment of glory or defeat, I am there.

TYLER WRAGE
Jesuit High School
Tampa, Florida

How Many Times?

Lord,
How many times have I sat here and realized how blessed
  I am, and how many times have I gone back to being
  the same person that I was before?

How many times have I stood in awe before the beauty of
  your creation and then turned around and defaced it?

How many times have I seen your immense love for me,
  and how many times have I rejected that love?

As many times as you have forgiven me in your
  infinite compassion, O Lord.

MATT SCHAEFFER
Jesuit High School
Sacramento, California

MY FRIEND

I have this friend;
I can talk to him,
And he will listen.
I can show him things,
He will watch.
I can ask for help,
And he'll most definitely help.
But, I can't see him!
But, then again, I can!
If I could ask him a question,
What would it be?
"Where can I find you?"
He answers—
shhhhhh, the man is whispering—
"Through people, nature, and yourself!"
This man is truly my best friend.
This man is Jesus!
Who is Jesus for me?
Jesus is my hero—
A man who guides me
Through thick and thin
To follow that right path to sunshine.
What more could you ask from a friend?

MARTY HUBER
St. Xavier High School
Cincinnati, Ohio

Life Is Hard

Lord, my life seems very hard.
Every day I struggle at school
To make good grades, enjoy life, and still see you.
But if I would just take a moment to look around,
I would see that my life is not so harsh.
I pray, Lord, that you help me see
Beyond what is in front of me;
To see the good things in my life
And the obstacles for others,
So that I may help
To make your world a little better.
Amen.

CHRIS FRYER
Strake Jesuit College Preparatory
Houston, Texas

Make Your Life a Prayer

I woke up one day with a desire.
I thought I was the only one who could lift me higher.
Then I found out I was wrong.
There's only one dream worth holding on.

Now God gives us two ways to love.
Love someone down here and love him up above.
Let your love be your light
And let your heart decide what is right.

I woke one day with a desire lifting me higher.
I thought I was the only one but I found out I was wrong.
There's no hideout from his love.
It's going to find you no matter what.

Make your life a prayer.
Stare it straight in the face
And say, "This is why I'm here."
Make your life a prayer.
Keep it in its place
And say, "This is why I'm here."

JOHN GRIGAITIS IV
DeSmet Jesuit High School
St. Louis, Missouri

MaKe ME a SolDieR oF YouR PEaCe

Dear God,
I beg for your mercy. Help me to help the less fortunate and understand that when I help one of your people, I help you. Motivate me to make an effort in helping people with whatever they need. Remove the greed that consumes my heart and let me donate things to people who really could use them. Mend my heart to be a soldier of your army, striving to help the less fortunate, or plainly, just anyone in need. Keep your hands over me as I try to be a kind and loving person. Fill my heart with joy from helping others, and keep me in your footsteps. Give me a sound mind to work with people who truly need my help in any way. Let me be willing to sacrifice for others when it is possible. Amen.

DANIEL GOMEZ
Loyola High School of
  Los Angeles
Los Angeles, California

COME, HOLY SPIRIT

In the first letter of John, it is written,
   "The way we know we remain in Him and He in us
   is that He has given us His Spirit."

Heavenly Father,
As we celebrate your gift of the Holy Spirit, grant us
wisdom, that we may aspire after those things which are
eternal; understanding, that our minds may be filled with
your divine truth; counsel, that we may choose the surest
way of gaining heaven; fortitude, that we, too, may bear
your cross; knowledge, that we may know you, and in turn
ourselves; piety, that we find the service of you necessary;
and fear, that we may be filled with loving reverence for you.

MIKE HUDE
Brophy College Preparatory
Phoenix, Arizona

WHeRe LiFe NEveR ENds

Neverending dream where life never ends—
  Where people live in perfect harmony,
  Where color is not wrong,
  Where we can walk and sing without
    laughter of putdowns,
  Where someone greets you with words of joy,
  Where loneliness and inequality become a speck of
    dirt in the winds of the past—
But reality must come first.

JEFF WHITE BEAR CLAWS
Red Cloud Indian School
Pine Ridge, South Dakota

Give Me

Dear God,
Give me the strength to love others and to be loved.
Guide me through each day with your helping hand.
Give me the knowledge that you are always there,
Especially when I need you the most.
Give me the courage to live each moment
  as if the next will never come.
Show me how to be strong when I am feeling weak.
Give me the strength to live as you intended me to.
Amen.

CASSIE KOBERTS
Brebeuf Jesuit College
Preparatory School
Indianapolis, Indiana

PRioRiTieS

Lord, why do I allow my schoolwork and how well I do in
  chemistry or calculus on a certain day to control my mood?
  I get frustrated so easily if I don't understand something
  in class, and I develop a somber, angry attitude.
Thank you for having kept me right-minded up until now.
Jesus, please console me and put my heart at ease.
Allow me to create a healthy balance between
  school, sports, and fun,
And to always have you as my first priority
  in all areas of my life.

JOE BOMMARITO
St. Louis University High School
St. Louis, Missouri

Prayer for Compassion

Please Lord
Grant me not the ability to think compassionately
Nor the knowledge to know that I can love
Nor the ability to change the world
Give me the faith
The courage
And the understanding that compassion without action
That knowledge of love without accomplishments
And the ability to change the world without dedication
Is utterly useless
Instill your verities in me
As well as your *mas maiorem*
Let me be your mouthpiece
Let me be your . . .
Companion

MATTHEW PEREZ
Xavier High School
New York, New York

PRaYeR foR HeLp TO RaISE MY GRaDeS

Dear God,

> Strengthen my memory,
> Sharpen my focus,
> Energize my concentration,
> Give me the necessary discipline,
> Aid my understanding,
> Increase my comprehension,
> Remind me to be inquisitive,
> Enhance my academic powers,
> And if it be your will, help me raise my grades.

I promise to remember that all my achievements

> Are your blessings

And are possible only through your grace.
I promise to give you all the glory.

TREY TOLLE
Jesuit High School
New Orleans, Louisiana

Enséñame

¿De qué sirve poseer conocimiento y sabiduría
Si aun no puedo ser feliz?
Conozco y soy capaz de mencionar los secretos del triunfo,
Pero no los puedo vivir.
Señor, Enséñame a reconocer mis imperfecciones.
Hazme receptivo a tu verdad
Y pon a un lado mi orgullo y vanidad.

Señor, ilumíname.
Que yo, por mucho que creo saber,
Tengo solo un mediocre conocimiento de las cosas.
Hazme humilde,
Ya que mi experiencia y sapiencia de palabras hermosas
Es inútil
Si no hace nada para promover tu Palabra.

Señor, lléname.
Para que, en la quieta soledad de mi vida,
Descubra la Paz perfecta que es tu amor
Y encuentre satisfacción en mi propio entendimiento de tu ser.

Señor, guíame.
Para que a traves de mi hablar y mis escrituras
Me haga el proclamador de Amor
Que ha podido asimilar y vivir en soledad.
No pido nada más, Señor.
Enséñame.

TEach ME (translation of "Enséñame")

What is the purpose of possessing knowledge and wisdom
If I cannot be happy?
I find myself aware of and able to share the secrets of triumph,
But I cannot live by them.
Lord, teach me to recognize my imperfections.
Make me susceptible to your truth
And put aside my pride and vanity.

Lord, enlighten me.
For I, as much as I may think I know,
Have but a mediocre grasp of things.
Humble me,
For my fondness for and knowledge of beautiful words
Is useless
If it does nothing to promote your Word.

Lord, fill me
So that I, in the quiet solitude of my life,
May discover the perfect peace that is your love
And be satisfied by my own understanding of you.

Lord, guide me
So that through my speech and my writings
I may become the proclaimer of Love
Who has been able to assimilate and live in peace.
I ask for nothing else, Lord.
Teach me.

ELSA MUNOZ
St. Ignatius College Prep
Chicago, Illinois

PRAYER FOR DIRECTION

Through bad times in Egypt,
Through the wilderness into the Promised Land,
You have led us.

Through everyday conflict,
Through everyday troubles,
You lead us.

Through all that will come before us,
Through all that may threaten us,
You will lead us.

You have led us.
You lead us now.
You will lead us in the future.
You never forsake us; help us not to forsake you.

AMIT SANGAVE
McQuaid Jesuit High School
Rochester, New York

THe RoSe

Red, pink, white, yellow
Numerous colors, the rainbow and more
An extravagant reminder of what God gave us

But the source of this rose comes through the thorns
That beautiful rose hurts those who reach for it

The thorns are Jesus' life, his story
For us he suffered and died
For us he bled his rosy red blood

The rose is a symbol of faith
The pain and agony it took to bring out the beauty of God
Those thorns opened the gates of heaven
The rose buds, exposing its color

Lord, remind me when I pick up a rose of your creation
Discard the beauty; the thorns are my foundation

ANDREW DAVIS
Fairfield College
    Preparatory School
Fairfield, Connecticut

CiRCLe oF THaNKs

Lord,
Thank you for my life,
For without my life,
I could never enjoy my family and my friends.
Thank you for my family and my friends,
For without my family and friends
I could never enjoy happiness.
Thank you for my happiness,
For without my happiness, I could never enjoy a smile.
Thank you for a smile,
For without a smile I could never enjoy life.
Amen.

EMILY HASENSTAB
Walsh Jesuit High School
Cuyahoga Falls, Ohio

LIKE YOUR SON

Dear Lord,
Thank you for giving us life and love.
Give us all strength to live our lives
And to love one another.
Give us the inner peace to admit when we
Are wrong and to mend a quarrel.
Give us the courage to forgive one another,
And most important,
Give us the strength to be more like your son
So that we can put others first.
Amen.

KATIE SCHWENK
Brebeuf Jesuit College
Preparatory School
Indianapolis, Indiana

Prayer of Awakening

Pray I that these harpist winds my ears
Do comprehend; pray I that first light's
Painted sky my eyes retain for soul's
Piercing gaze, breaking shell of sense's
Blue. Now sings all eternal tune, lost
Song of origin in riddle without,
So melodious within it plays of
God! Awakened, my vision once more,
As sounds divine flutter into space; away
To make Creator's image (I blinded
To it no more) of all that walks or
Rests subtly.

All failure this morn, all
Common things, now dressed in robes, in
White: angelic, unfailing, godly;
Truths of realm unseen glimmer as soul's
Pure ray enlightens a fog-coated
Land of childish wonder, undying
But deplored by reason, ailment
Of world growing in all save deathless
Part, the only that shall flourish at
Body's fail and tower's crumble; at
Ethereal stand over the fated sensual
Being we and world are not; nor shall

We plunge to such deplorable trap,
To shackles of an empty day, to
Chemist's bland totality, while God
Enters Sunday temple in horrid
Formality.

But holy prayer
Ceaseless beats on through the time of toil,
The harp sounds on in beggar's voice, in
Kingly day, in country hut, in most
Grand vale, in ecstasy, in sorrow's
Wail, in all that once seemed truth with
No beyond, no within. Now a soul
Has filled my eyes, kindled is a flame
Within, unquenchable; a soul that
Sees its fiery self in all that was
Once dormant coal, as was I when
But a frame in my own failing eyes,
Those that see myself in all; the atoms
Were once all around, but now God's ever
Glory my soul does view, here and there,
Within me always and within you!

NICHOLAS D. BUDNIEWSKI
Canisius High School
Buffalo, New York

WHeN I FaiL

I have seen
What I know,
I feel
Much more than
I know I know.
I have shown
What I have,
I have given
Much less than
I have had.
I have stood up for
Those things I cherish,
I have retreated,
Or compromised in heart,
Much more than
I have stood for.

So when I fail—to know, to give, or to protect—
Forgive me.

JOE BYRON
Georgetown Preparatory School
North Bethesda, Maryland

AT GEtHsEmaNi AbbEy's DooR

I entered the church
More or less a normal church
The monks faced each other
A gate separated us

And then they sang . . .
Their voices resonating
In the presence of God
Praising him beyond anything
I had ever experienced

And then they bowed before his altar . . .
Their hands down to their feet
Humility, vulnerability
Announcing subservience
Love . . .

"Praise to the Father, the Son
And the Holy Spirit
Both now and forever
The God who is
Who was
And who is to come
At the end of the ages."

MATT KORFHAGEN
St. Xavier High School
Cincinnati, Ohio

WHY?

True friends only come a few times in a lifetime;
They listen, they help, they play.
Memories are all I have.
But there is no logical reason as to why,
Other than that someone in the sky is in charge.
But why intervene?
Why take a piece of my childhood?
It is not fair.

You watch the life around you,
The meaningless things that cloud your mind,
The unreal thing that happens wipes all of these things
from your mind.
You think how, when, where.
But I am a man of logic
So I ask why,
In this lifetime, I question,
Why are you here to do this?
Tell me God, he was only sixteen,
I don't understand how you work.

Life is so precious,
Do we take it for granted?
You provide this world, this pain, this agony,
Why?
We live, we try, we fight, but God,
Why give this to us?
Most can handle it,
But those who cry inside at night,
Who show no emotion on the outside,
They need a hand to pull them out of the darkness,
They reach, and there is no response.
Why?
Why is there no response?

God, you have these plans for us.
What are they?
Why do we have them?
God, help me justify this tragedy.
If such a thing is possible, show me, tell me,
Is life worth sixteen years, to tempt and take away?

He was not married,
He did not have a family,
He did not get to pursue his dreams.
Why?
Why was he taken?
What did he do?
Did he deserve this?
What mysterious way do you work in?

God sits in the light,
Watching me fight through the dark world,
I suffer to reason why this world is like this,
But I need help,
So I ask,
God, why did you take him?

Dedicated to Marcus Ryan Gabbard,
From an unfortunate friend needing to ask

MICHAEL WEINGARTNER
Regis High School
New York, New York

Prayer to the Infant

Hush glorious child, beloved and near,
Ample of charity, gracious, and pure.
Primed for your fate, you compel us to the moral path,
Through a sinuous defile, both somber and long,
We follow your lead, and imitate your compassion.
Exposed and intrepid, you alone are the Lamb
To whom I owe my salvation.
Yours alone is the life
To which I strive to dedicate my every action.
And you alone shall I follow
From the clay of the earth, into the kingdom of heaven—
Or any place else you should lead.

BRAD FREEMAN
Boston College High School
Dorchester, Massachusetts

Hey Friend

Hey Friend! I saw you in
The crowds today. I called
Your name out, but you
Did not hear.
Hey Friend! I saw you on
The street today. I waved
To you, but you
Did not wave back.
Hey Friend! I saw you all
Alone today. I smiled at
You and said hi, but you
Did not look at me.
Hey Friend, I think I'll
Call you Stranger.

THERESE COUGHLIN
Loyola Academy
Wilmette, Illinois

CLOSING tHe GaP

Dear Lord,

Why is there sometimes a large gap between what I want and what I need? You almost always give me what I need and sometimes give me what I want. For that I am grateful.

I have noticed that what I need becomes what I want. This is when I become more dependent on you. I can never remember a time when you've ever let me down. I see even in the little things how you help me in my daily life. For that I am grateful.

I ask you to please help me choose correctly those things I need. I ask you to help me want less. There are so many others who need your help more than I do, but still you find time for me. Lord, I will always be grateful to you.

ANONYMOUS
St. John's Jesuit High School
Toledo, Ohio

WHAT HAS GOD BECOME?

Remember the prayers taught by our teachers?
The sermons spoken by the preachers?
We were taught to respect all God's creatures.
What has God become?

Inspiring us to change our lives,
Loving those whom we might despise,
Exclaiming the truth instead of explaining lies.
What has God become?

And sometimes I feel I've lost the fight,
But then there is this guiding light.
What has God become?

Trusting the light brings me home
From this place I will not roam.
It brings me a peace I have never known.
This is what God has become.

TIP KRESS
Marquette University
High School
Milwaukee, Wisconsin

Power to Pray

God, give me the willpower to talk with you,
To confide in you my fears,
To tell you my secrets,
To share with you my joys,
To weep to you my sorrows,
And to listen to your words of guidance.

God, also give me the knowledge to keep my prayer vital,
To try different ways of communicating with you,
To sit in your holy presence,
To bask in your perfection,
To float in your goodness,
And to be one with you throughout this life and in the next.
Amen.

ROSS B. NODURFT
Jesuit High School
New Orleans, Louisiana

A Student's Shema

Dear God,
Help me to love others just as Jesus did,
to see your divine image in them,
and to love you with all my mind, heart, and soul.
Amen.

HENRY DANAHER
Rockhurst High School
Kansas City, Missouri

FiNdiNG OuR SuNrise

Once it had set
we had no regret
Just the dark night
Oh the endless twilight

The air grew so cold,
but our moon made us so bold
and we fought our fight
how we conquered that night

Its beauty we craved
without which we are depraved
How foolish we had been
Our sunrise was all around and within

Now that we found our sunrise
We fear it is done
but with this sunrise
Our day has begun

Lord, help each of us find our sunrise,
and show us that we never lost it.

JOHN O'DONNELL
St. Joseph's Preparatory School
Philadelphia, Pennsylvania

First-Time Finals

Dear God,
Semester finals are coming soon. I am a freshman and have
never taken them before. My teachers tell me that it will
be a big part of my grade, and I'm kind of nervous about
it. My teachers have given me tons of information, and
I don't know if I will be able to memorize all of it. I don't
know even where to begin. There are some classes and
programs my parents want me to attend to help me out,
but I don't know if those will help me or if my parents are
just making me do more things. I have a few classes that
could either be passed or failed depending on the grade
I receive on my final. I am really nervous, Lord. Please help
me to study the right things and to get good grades.

CHRIS KENNALEY
Rockhurst High School
Kansas City, Missouri

THE CALL OF A GOOD SAMARITAN

Lord, teach me to be a good Samaritan
To help those in pain
To remember the forgotten
And to fight for justice
And teach me to give to the needy
To tend to those injured souls I find along my journey of life
And to forever live in the name of your son, Jesus.
Show me the way.
Teach me to be an unsung hero
Constantly enduring the toils of a life of justice.
Let me suffer with the lowly
And constantly offer the assistance
  that I would wish for myself.
Amen.

KYLE METZROTH
St. Xavier High School
Cincinnati, Ohio

PEaCe Is . . .

a handshake of understanding
an overture of diplomacy
a compromise of society
a finale to suffering
a plea for harmony
a chance for forgiveness
a truce of generosity
an end to animosity
an outburst of courage
a shadow of patience
a treaty of recognition
a stop to hatred
an occasion to rejoice
an option to believe in
a decision to trust one's enemies
an agreement to break barriers
an accord of serenity
a choice to live by one's faith
an appeal to accept differences
a conclusion to battle
an introduction to acceptance
a grateful display of diversity
an offer to disarm
an approach to greater strength
a show of self-confidence

an act of bravery
a reconciliation of violence
a disappearance of war
a performance of silence
a call to exiles
a return to friendship
an outstretched hand
a reason for hope
a shoulder of reliance
an assistance to those in need
a banishment of persecution
a guidance to refugees
an effect of loyalty
an uprooting of terror
a promise to live in safety
a shining star in a dark sky
a direction for the lost ones
a leader for the unguided
a story of success
a time for joy and happiness.
Peace is also
    an opportunity to find love in the world.

ANDY NOVAK
University of Detroit Jesuit
  High School and Academy
Detroit, Michigan

NeveR SHut YOuR EyeS

Help us listen to these words:
As Jesus is the sower, so are we the seeds.
Let his word be sown freely in all countries where prejudice
  and governments repress.
Guard it from the birds that will swallow it;
Keep it deep within our hearts so that the birds of our lives
  cannot find it.
Protect it within that haven from vices and temptations
  that so quickly confound it.
Let his word take firm root inside of us.
Don't just idly listen and think to ourselves
  how nice it all sounds,
And forget it all when our friends invite us over
  for the night.
Keep ourselves away from thorns: hard drugs,
  hate, violence.
Keep ourselves apart from these so that they don't choke
  the work when it is inside of us.
Keep our consciences free so that we will be ready to listen.
Most important, keep our ears and eyes always open,
Never shutting out new ideas or thoughts,
Never closing our minds or being stubborn,
Never listening only to what is comfortable or simple.

Based on Luke 8:4-8

JOHN ELFERS
St. Xavier High School
Cincinnati, Ohio

BeYoNd UnDeRstaNdinG

Energy that sustains my life,
Unknown power behind all,

How can I unwrap your mysteries,
Your hidden presence within all?

I do not know how you affect me,
Perhaps in more ways than I know,

And even when I think I've got it,
Another face of yours will show.

JOHN WITTING
Loyola Academy
Wilmette, Illinois

WHeRe?

War, death, murder, hate, racism, prejudice, disease, famine,
disaster. Where is the Being, the Lord, the Father, the Spirit,
God? Why is the world the way it is? Why the questions?
Why the agony? Where is God in all these things?
God is there . . . there in the hearts, souls, minds, and thoughts
Of those who stand against the world's pain, those who
Stand for peace, life, care, love, equality, cures, aid.
Lord, let me strive to be one of those messengers.

SHASHI K. DHOLUNDAS
St. Peter's Preparatory School
Jersey City, New Jersey

Sex: Learning the Hard Way

Above all else, I want to be honest in my relationships. From what I have experienced, I know there is no worse feeling in the entire world than knowing you've hurt the person you love. I had to learn the hard way what distrust can do to a relationship. I almost lost the person that meant more to me than anyone I've ever known. I not only lost my girlfriend, but I almost lost my best friend because I was dishonest. Please give me the strength to tell the truth, even when it may hurt. Please allow me to have the courage to stand up for what is right, no matter what the situation or the consequences. There is no greater way to display my love for someone than by letting them know that I will always be myself with them, not a person hiding behind a mask of deceit. When I love someone more than life itself, I know I have found someone to whom I am not afraid to tell the truth. Help me to be honest in everything I do, and with everyone I know, and most important, with the people I love.

MATT HAMMER
St. Xavier High School
Cincinnati, Ohio

Spring

In the sweet fluttering of apple blossoms
  you cascade around me,
        Dancing in front of my eyes . . .
          And . . .
        Landing in my hair . . .
          And . . .
        Pervading my senses
          With your
        Glistening scent . . .
          And . . .
        Soaring like butterflies . . .
        So that when I go home
          Hours later,
        I find white snowdrop petals
        Nestling in my clothes.

JULIA MATSON
Loyola Academy
Wilmette, Illinois

My Sanctuary

Lord, you are my sanctuary.
I dwell within your house,
And there I am safe.
You dwell within my soul,
And with you there I am safe.
Let me never neglect your house,
Oh Lord.
Let me never neglect my soul,
Oh Lord, let me never neglect you.

RYAN HARRIS
St. Louis University High School
St. Louis, Missouri

CHeRisH

Dear Lord,
help us to cherish
every day,
every hour,
every moment,
and every second.
Teach us to be thankful for everything we have been
blessed with, especially that which we take for granted
everyday. Help us to reach out to others who may not
have as much as we do, and to be patient with those
who may cause us grief. Help us to remember that there
are other people who are going through the same sort of
things that we are, and that we can overcome these obstacles.

CHRIS DOLL
Jesuit High School
Tampa, Florida

PRaYeR foR LiFe

We thank you, heavenly Father, for the most precious gift of life. Help us to cherish and respect this gift. Enable us to help those in our society whose lives and health are threatened and attacked by abortion, poverty, neglect, abuse, and ignorance. Where we find these assaults on your great gift of life, let us be your messengers of help and hope to those who are threatened. Let us pray with St. Ignatius Loyola that we might be able to "give to those in need and not to count the cost, to fight for justice and not to heed the wounds, and to labor in the cause of life and to ask for no reward save that of knowing that in this work we do your will." Amen.

PRO-LIFE COMMITTEE
DeSmet Jesuit High School
St. Louis, Missouri

PRaYeR foR tHe JoUrNeY

Dear God,

Please help me to remember that the most important thing in my life is to be a good person. My main goal in life is to get to heaven. Sometimes I forget this simple fact. Many times I think of school or my future job as the most important thing. Lord, please help me to keep my eyes on you. If I remember my main goal, then I will avoid the small sins commonly committed by my peers: swearing, lying, and insulting others. Please give me the graces to combat temptation. Furthermore, please help me to remember to read the Bible, the blueprint for the Christian faith. If I read your word every day, I know that I will be a better person spiritually.

In Jesus Christ's name,
Amen.

FEDERIC MAK
Loyola High School of
  Los Angeles
Los Angeles, California

BaGGaGE

Loving God,
Our fears and anxieties, our worries and stresses, and our
pain and suffering are all unnecessary baggage. Let us lose
this burdensome weight and free ourselves to the
possibilities of love and hope.

BOYD DENNINGTON
Brophy College Preparatory
Phoenix, Arizona

FOR THE EARTH

Dear God,
You are full of power and glory.
You created a world on which it was suitable
for life to live and thrive.
Before technology arose,
this world that you created was pure.
Since then, we as the people inhabiting Earth
have dirtied our waters, polluted our air,
and littered our land.
As the pollution of this world increases,
so too does the tainting of the beautiful
environment which you created.
As we burn up our fossil fuels and cut down trees,
More and more species of animals, insects, and plants
begin to die off at alarming rates.
Help us to see the error of our ways,
and give us the patience to fix some of our mistakes.
Amen.

JASON KIRCHEN
Loyola High School of
Los Angeles
Los Angeles, California

EveRyDaY PRaYeR

Dear God,
Please hear this prayer and listen to it.
This prayer is for the weak, the disabled, and the poor:
May they be safe, strong, and full of happiness;
May they know no troubles that they can't surmount.
Please help the strong, proud, and rich:
May they be humble servants of God and help others.
Will you please pray for all of humankind:
Whether we are white, black, tall, short, fat, or skinny,
Help us to follow your word and reject the devil and his
friends;
May we be strong in fighting for your sake;
May we never shy away from helping, saving,
and caring for someone less or more
Fortunate than we are.
Please hear our prayer, and act on it.
We pray in your son's name,
Jesus Christ.
Thank you God for hearing our prayer.

DREW LACY
Loyola Blakefield
Towson, Maryland

Sometimes
I Am Confused, Lord

I am confused about a lot of things, but most of the time
   I am confused about your existence.
My mind wants a good hard answer that makes sense,
   but there is really no hard answer that we know of.
I wonder how you got here and where you came from.
I think and think and think, but I can never find
   the right answer that satisfies my imagination.
Please help me to understand that it is not important
   to know where you came from, but it is important
   to understand and appreciate everything
   that you have done for me.
Through your guidance, Lord, help me to understand more
   about your existence and how much you love me. Amen.

PAT BEFORT
Rockhurst High School
Kansas City, Missouri

God's Garden

Lord, make me your forest,
    Filled with strong, healthy trees
To shelter the birds
    In the wintertime.
Let me be long, green grass to feed
    The animals.
Let me be a stream of fresh water
    So all creatures can drink,
And let me be cooling shade to refresh
    The earth in the heat of summer.

TANYA CLIFFORD
Red Cloud Indian School
Pine Ridge, South Dakota

CHRISTMAS PRAYER

O Lord, as we prepare for your birthday,
Please take care of your children,
Especially those less fortunate than we are.
Please remind us of the true meaning of Christmas,
Which is to appreciate the blessings you have given us,
And to give rather than to receive.
Lord, also remind us how to live as Christians
By living our lives the way you did,
Which means to treat one another
  as we would like to be treated.
And finally, Lord, please especially bless my family,
  my friends, my relatives, and me
This Christmas because around this time of year we need
All the extra strength you can give us.
Thank you, Lord, and happy birthday.
Amen.

TOMMY SMITH
Xavier High School
New York, New York

THE FUTURE

Bless the art education with the Holy Spirit
For these children are the future of your kingdom on earth.
The fate of your creation lies in their hands;
Make those hands gentle, O Lord,
That they may cradle the world.
Now and forever,
Amen.

TONY CASUBOLO
Fairfield College
Preparatory School
Fairfield, Connecticut

Prayer for Justice

O God, there are so many problems in the world today.
People hate each other everywhere, and for every reason.
Racism, Sexism, Ageism—all kinds of discrimination exist.
War seems to erupt in new places everyday—
    and for what reason?
Why can't there be a just world, a world
    where these problems don't exist?
Jesus, help me not only to understand why,
    but also help me to make a change.
I want to make a difference in this world—help me.

MATTHEW BROWNE
Boston College High School
Dorchester, Massachusetts

One God . . . One People

Today people separate because of religion,
For neither side can take any type of criticism.
One must mark down on a standardized test,
Whether their blood comes from Jerusalem,

  Mecca, Rome, or Tibet.
Well, I say it's time to take down the bars,
Placing an end to all religious wars.
If everyone today who reads this poem
Accepts others' differences,
All could live in complete harmony.
I pray to you, almighty Lord, please let this be.

TRAVIS MANDELL
St. John's Jesuit High School
Toledo, Ohio

PRaYeR foR EnDuRanCe

Lord, help me to endure,
> Even when I think I have nothing left.
> Show me how to finish what I start.
> And let me live as your son.
> Jesus showed me this.

JAKE LENNON
St. Xavier High School
Cincinnati, Ohio

PRAYER FOR THOSE WHO STUMBLE

Dear Lord, my God and Savior, please help me as I stumble through this, your world. Many things confuse me. Forgive my sins, and assist me in not committing more. Drive me to succeed, but not so much that I hurt those around me. And watch over those I love, whether living or in your kingdom. I pray these things through Jesus Christ, your son. Amen.

ADAM MEYERS
Rockhurst High School
Kansas City, Missouri

Family Prayer

Dear God,
Thank you for everything you have given me.
Thank you for my life, my friends, and my family.
Thank you for giving me a stepfather—
   a stepfather to take the place of my real father
   who doesn't bother to care.
Thank you for giving me a little brother
   to love and take care of.
You have given me a chance to be a role model
   for my brother like my dad never was for me.
God, please give me the strength to forgive
   and for us to love one another as equals.
Please help the people in need of food, shelter,
   love, and security.
Through Christ our Lord. Amen.

MONTAE PERKINS
Rockhurst High School
Kansas City, Missouri

IT'S ME AGAIN

Dear God,
I know I ask a lot of you, but it's me again.
I'm just looking for the comfort of a friend.
I ask you now to watch over and guide me.
Please help me and always stay right beside me.
If I'm in trouble and begin to lose it all,
I pray that you'll be right there to break my fall.
I ask you to look over my loved ones that have died,
I know that they are in good hands with you in the sky.
And if I ever lose faith and begin to doubt you,
Help me realize that I wouldn't be here without you.
So I ask you now to bless all my peers and me.
Look after me, and I will keep praying, all of my years.
Amen.

VINCE GALLAGHER
St. Joseph's Preparatory School
Philadelphia, Pennsylvania

WHAT IF ABRAHAM CAME TO OUR SCHOOL?

What if Abraham came to our school,
Just for a day, to speak?
If Abraham came and looked at you and me,
would he be happy with what he saw?
Would he be satisfied with just our grades?
Or would he inquire about our souls?
He wouldn't let us off with only a partial effort.
He would tell us about the *magis,*
Striving for more in everything we do.
But what made Abraham's life such a success?
And what made his descendants successes, too?
They were successes because they took God's hand.
Even when they faltered and sinned,
God didn't turn his back on them,
And when they died they were buried
in the Promised Land.

What is the moral of these parables?
Does God want us to do evil and break his trust?
No, but God does forgive, and when we make errors,
he will set us back on the right path.
His arms are always extended towards us,
with his palms turned upward toward the sky.
All we have to do is take his hand,
and we can become heroes, too,
Shedding our old selves as we depart,
Then becoming fulfilled,
And returning reborn and more mature.
God wants us to be heroes,
God wants us to be just,
And all we have to do to be heroes is not break his trust.

BOB BOREK
St. Xavier High School
Cincinnati, Ohio

Maestro for a Night

If I were the maestro for a night,
Oh, what joy there'd be!
I'd casually hang onto each and every liberating key.

To the stars I'd have to leave the dreaming,
And for the present, well . . . I'd stand up tall,
For the night would be for me—No, for all!

Love would drift right through my soul,
Satiating an unspeakable desire.
Thus within this I shall conclude, and unto sleep retire.

Then they'll come and guide me away,
But I'd scramble for each note with all my might,
For I'd be the maestro of this frenzied yet tranquil night.

JOHN GLEASON
Loyola Academy
Wilmette, Illinois

Prayer for the Poor

Oh God in heaven, and all saints,
I pray this prayer for someone in need.
It is not for me, but for those who
Need guidance, hope, and wisdom.
The earth is full of the rich, the wealthy, and the comfortable,
But far more numerous are the impoverished.
Please, oh heavenly Father,
Listen to this prayer for them.
They live worse than the animals of the wild.
They are rejected, and scorned by society.
Give them hope,
So that they may realize their worth and look for the best.
Give them guidance,
To help them to search for their own comfort.
Above all, give them wisdom,
So they know that they are loved.
Please Lord,
Influence those who are well-off to give aid.
Open their unseeing eyes,
And destroy their selfishness.
They turn their backs; they are wounds in earth's side.
Please give these gifts to those struck by poverty,
And help us to help them.
Amen.

LUKE STAGG
Saint Peter's Preparatory School
Jersey City, New Jersey

Your Life Is so Sweet

You only live once, they told me,
So make the best of every day, right?
You cannot change the life you're in,
So try to not let it go dim.
You have a special gift . . . life,
And it goes by swift . . . full of strife,
But your life is a special one
Because you are the only person who decides when it's done.
No other being has a life like yours,
That is why it's so special in your endeavors.
You make your life so sweet,
But I am the one who can make it complete.
They also say to laugh, cry, and love,
But I say to live and be like a dove.
Just to fly to the heavens above
Is a feeling no one else can think of.

Your life is special because no one else has one like it,
That is why it's a perfect fit.
Within your life, there will be trauma and happiness,
But remember: I will always be there even through the stress.
Life is so sweet,
And I make it complete.
Respect all the people around you;
Love all who you want to;
But remember I am here to inspire
'Cause my love for everyone is hotter than fire.
This is my message to you . . . that your life is so sweet,
But never forget you have to live to make it complete.

Peace, Hope, Love, Knowledge

JON CAMPBELL
Jesuit High School
Tampa, Florida

HeLL

There are no safe harbors in hell
People are people
And people want other people around
But they aren't there
Words are scorched white
They've dried up in the sun
Like the dream these people used to have
They are drowning here
In pools of guilt, fear, isolation
They are surrounded by others
But still alone
That loneliness is the worst kind
Feeling outside of it all
Knowing you have something to give
But unable to do so
Imprinted black amid a sea of blue
Wondering how it would feel to die

Picturing the scene
Living the scene outside your mind
But unable to act
Unable to change at all
Living there in a blue/green room
Staring at the ceiling for support
Calling out a way to communicate
But words hang like ghosts
Inside
The green is up in flames
Moving like drunken clouds
Choking out those around them
Still hell is always living
And never being able to die

MICHAEL YEAGER
St. Xavier High School
Cincinnati, Ohio

Always with Us

To what place can I go, God, where I'm not
   inside your creation?
            How could I possibly run away from you?
            If I climb the highest mountain,
            you are with me still.
If I swim to the bottom of the ocean, you are with me still.
            If I attempt to hide from you, you are with me still.
            If I move to a distant land, you are with me still.
Even in these difficulties, you will reveal your path.
            Even in struggles you will lead me to yourself,
      From whom I had never truly departed at all.

Adapted from Psalm 139: 7-10

NICHOLAS INALATA
Loyola High School of
   Los Angeles
Los Angeles, California

Bless Us

God, please bless us with a need to respect others
   and ourselves.
Bless us with forgiveness that we may forgive others
   who do wrong against us, or those whom we hurt
   in any way.
Bless us with the power of love in all we do, in all we say.
Bless us that we may gain a better education,
   a better understanding of what we are learning.
Bless us with honesty, understanding, and compassion
   that we may be honest with others and ourselves.
Bless us with all these things. To you we are thankful.

PEGGY NOT HELP HIM
Red Cloud Indian School
Pine Ridge, South Dakota

More Than an Accident

Dear Lord,

As I reflect upon the natural wonders of the world around me, it is hard to understand how science can say it is all just a result of an accidental cosmic explosion. When I look around and see all these sights, I cannot believe that all of this incredible beauty came into being by chance. When I look at the endless variety of plants and animals, I know it must be the work of your hands. If I ever start to think that you do not care, or even consider that you are not there, I will go out and look at your creation and remember that it is all part of your grand design.

KEVIN ZEILER
Loyola Blakefield
Towson, Maryland

FaiTh iN GoD

Faith in God for life,
Dealing with problems and with strife.
Stress of school and trials with friends
Are what push us to our ends.
That little boy I helped last week
Makes me wonder why the other child didn't turn his cheek.
God, you work in a mysterious way
Giving me the courage and grace to say
I forgive my friend and hope for the best,
And to you, Lord, I leave the rest.

JEFF SYKORA
Fairfield College
   Preparatory School
Fairfield, Connecticut

PRAYER FOR THE CONTINUING OF CREATION

In the beginning stood primeval history,
And the story of creation rests still as a mystery.
Yet let there be light, was the word of God,
And thus came forever, an end to the dark.

The heavens were open,
And down came his gifts: a shower of water, land, and bliss.
And upon the earth he placed vegetation,
With every fruit and seed, to set to migration.

Next came the cattle, the birds, and the trees,
And the creatures of the oceans, as they rest in the seas.
In the image of God, came human beings,
With the start of them being Adam and Eve.

Six days have passed, and God's work is now done.
Yet the story of creation has only begun.
Amen.

JULIAN SELTZER
Boston College High School
Dorchester, Massachusetts

IMaGeS

Up in the clouds, behind a golden gate,
God sat brightly determining my fate.
With a long white robe and a thick gray beard,
One careless sin and it was hell I feared.

Making a list and checking it twice,
I'm expecting a lot since I've been extra nice.
Doing good deeds is its own reward,
That's why I prayed for what I can't afford.

Another day goes by, and things aren't going my way,
So I kneel down, close my eyes, and I begin to pray.
It seems I only turn to God when things are going wrong;
I pray for guidance to guide me through, and strength
  to make me strong.

With every act of kindness, every dirty look,
God has it written down in his big record book.
Destiny is determined among the pages,
Life recorded throughout the ages.

Who do these images of God represent?
He is not a storybook God, a Santa Claus God,
  an aspirin God, nor an accountant.
Understand that God is in every tear and every smile you see.
God is in you, and God is in me.

STEFANIE LINARES
Loyola Academy
Wilmette, Illinois

A Prayer for Mental Strength

When times get rough and I stress out,
Lord, enter my mind and calm me down.
Give me the strength to focus and concentrate,
And to do the best that I can,
And more.

Give me peace and help me in making decisions.
Lead me to the right choice.
I really want to succeed,
But I am still nervous and scared.

I know the material.
Shepherd me from stupid mistakes.
Give me the power to triumph.
I know I can.
I know I will.
I know that with you at my side,
I am bound to persevere.

TIP KRESS
Marquette University
High School
Milwaukee, Wisconsin

A Prayer for the Outcast

Dear God,
I often feel I am hated by all and singled out as a loser.
Help me to stand strong in times like these.
Help me to forgive those who persecute me,
For I am weak, and I may not be able to do this on my own.
Help me to seek the truth in all matters and to stand up
  for what I believe in,
Even if it means almost certain rejection by my peers.
Help me and those like me to bear this together.

ANONYMOUS
Jesuit High School
New Orleans, Louisiana

Prayer for Guidance in Times of Indecision

Dear God,
I come to you with much indecision,
   and pray for your guidance.
Life is like a tandem bicycle in this way:
Too many times I sit in front and steer,
and ask you to pedal as hard as you can.
I try to enforce my own will, and ask you
   to help keep me safe on the way through.
Sometimes you become an object of convenience;
I think of you only when I'm in trouble,
   and for that I have much sorrow.
God, please help me stop, climb off the bike,
   and switch places with you.
Let me pedal hard while you guide the way.
Let me keep focus, and stay with you always.
I ask this through Christ the Lord.

MATT McKIBBIN
Rockhurst High School
Kansas City, Missouri

Prayer for Social Justice Workers

God, I honor those working for social justice in the world.
God, give them courage to live out your mission,
for their fight is long and hard without much hope.

God, give them the strength to do what is right,
and to inspire others to follow your mission
as you lived it here on earth through Jesus.

God, allow them to teach us that
hate and oppression are not the answer.
Let them show us that only through love and mutual
respect can we achieve true justice for all on this earth.

God, I say this prayer to you in the hope that all people
on this earth can one day be treated with
compassion, respect, and love.

GEORGE GRIFFIN
St. Peter's Preparatory School
Jersey City, New Jersey

Prayer for a Peaceful Death

Death hurts.
Death hurts in a different way than other hurts.
It is overwhelming and inescapable.
I feel the pain upon discovering that a friend has died.
I feel the pain when my busy thoughts
  keep me from sleeping.
I feel the pain as I try to put death behind me
  and function again.
Time eases the pain;
Frustration and anger fade to calmness and understanding.
I move forward with restored strength in my heart.
I remind myself that they will never hurt again.

ANONYMOUS
St. Louis University
  High School
St. Louis, Missouri

Prayer for Wisdom

O good and gracious God who has power over all things,
  I ask you now to grant me wisdom,
  To know and accept myself as I am;
    Grant me discipline,
    To achieve self-control;
    And grant me peace,
  To possess calm in my mind as well as my heart.
    These I ask of you, O Lord.
      Amen.

JOHN KREBS
Rockhurst High School
Kansas City, Missouri

Living by Scripture

When reading the Bible, these are the lessons I take with me:
Follow God's commands and let God be your king.
God doesn't judge on appearance or position.
Nothing ever comes to those who aren't challenged.
Things aren't appreciated until they are gone.
Solemnity can soothe an agitated spirit.
Small bands that are passionate can defeat all the masses.
God can live and love with the lowliest and the least.
Jealousy isn't a characteristic of a champion.
Friends will be there when trouble arises.
Don't linger around evil.
Leave at the sight of trouble.
Never lay a hand on anyone.
God will supply us with what we need.
Take responsibility for your sins.
With God on your side, you will prosper.
Rejoice always; you are in God's presence.
Don't succumb to temptations, however lavish
   they may appear.
If you have done harm to another, ask for forgiveness.
Never come to doing evil because of evil done to you.

   Dear Lord,
      Always remind me of what I have learned in Scripture.
         Amen.

ANDREW McEVOY
St. Xavier High School
Cincinnati, Ohio

THe CaLL

I fall under my burden and claim defeat.
I let the world pass me by,
And I lie in the darkness,
Brought low by the weight on my shoulders.
I give up, and I do nothing;
But then I feel a push from behind,
Gentle at first, but growing ever stronger.
As I am lifted up, some of my burden is taken
By my unseen companion.
The push continues to grow,
Forcing me out of the darkness
And not just into the world,
But into a position to lead it.
It is only then that I turn,
And see that you,
My friend,
Are the one who stayed behind
To lift me up,
When the world had forsaken me
And I had forsaken myself.
For this I thank you.
For this I love you.
For you I lead.

MATT REEDER
St. Xavier High School
Cincinnati, Ohio

Help Me

Help me, Lord, to do your will.
Help me to follow your words, even when it is difficult.
Teach me the things I will need to learn.
Help me to live a good life.

Help me, Lord, to be a good friend.
Teach me to be strong and not follow the crowd.
Help me to be kind to everyone.
Teach me to be honest, sincere, and trustworthy.

Help me, Lord, to be a good student.
Teach me to pay attention in class and study.
Help me to work to my ability and not cheat myself.
Teach me to be dedicated, conscientious, and earnest.

Help me, Lord, to be a good athlete.
Teach me to train hard and often.
Help me to give my best to the coach and the team.
Teach me to be fair, sportsmanlike, and team oriented.

Help me, Lord, to be a good son.
Teach me to obey my parents and do what is right.
Help me to practice the values I have been taught.
Teach me to be considerate, obedient, and helpful.

Help me, Lord, to be a good brother.
Teach me not to be jealous of others' accomplishments.
Help me to share my things and to do my share.
Teach me to be a family member, a partner, and a friend.

Help me, Lord, to be a good Catholic.
Teach me to be proud of my faith and practice it always.
Help me to keep God's laws, even when it is not easy.
Teach me to be pious, humble, and devout.

Help me, Lord, to do your will.
Help me to follow your words, even when it is difficult.
Teach me the things I will need to learn.
Help me to live a good life.

CHRIS BLUDGUS
St. Peter's Preparatory School
Jersey City, New Jersey

JEaLOUSY

Dear Lord,
Help me to understand my talents and my gifts. Do not
let my eyes stray from your path by envying those abilities
and opportunities that others possess. Let jealousy be
unable to deter me and let joy take its place. Guide me
in a direction that will allow me to enjoy others'
accomplishments and talents. Show me how to be proud of
them and to encourage them wholeheartedly. Do not let
jealous rage get the best of me. Let me see how truly
special I am to you. Thank you.

CHRIS FINNEY
St. Louis University
High School
St. Louis, Missouri

WHeN ALL SeeMS IMpossibLe

Dear God,

There are some mornings when waking up for school seems impossible. All I want to do is roll over and go back to sleep. Then I think of the day ahead of me, and I realize how lucky I am to go to school and see all of my friends.

I know that sometimes I become frustrated with my loved ones, but the truth is that they mean the world to me. Lord, please help me show my friends just how grateful I am to have them. They are always by my side and I honestly do not know how I could go through life without them. They fill my days with laughter and excitement. The amazing thing is that I can always be myself when I am with them. Thank you for blessing me with such wonderful friendships, and especially for being my greatest friend.

FRAN ROTELLA
St. Peter's Preparatory School
Jersey City, New Jersey

It'd All Be Worth It

Please be with me today.
Give me the courage to stand for and do what's right.
Help me to change the things I can,
To accept what I can't change,
And the wisdom to know the difference.
Anoint me with your power
That I might make a difference for you.

If I might make one person's day,
It'd all be worth it.
If I could be there in just one person's need,
It'd all be worth it.
If I could put a smile on just one face,
It'd all be worth it.
If I could be a shoulder for just one person to cry on,
It'd all be worth it.

Thank you for the blessings and gifts
that are present in my life
Each and every day.
Amen.

JAMIE GRANT
Jesuit High School
Tampa, Florida

THE NEXT STEP

How does one say good-bye
To a world they've always known,
And begin what's called a future,
To symbolize how much they have grown?

The road to tomorrow is a scary thing
That many are intimidated to take,
But with your lending hand in mine
The solidarity will be sure to break.

Pictures and letters I take with me
So as to recollect my childhood past.
Memories are what I need to move on
For high school has gone so fast.

I ask for you to guide me
For on my two feet is where I'll be
Without my friends and family I love
Who I'll seldom get to see.

After eighteen years of life thus far
There's a world out there I never knew;
But with your hand to calm my fears,
I know I'll make it through.

LIZA VELAZCO
Loyola Academy
Wilmette, Illinois

PRAYER foR RiGhT RELATiONSHiPS

Dear Lord, thank you for family and friends.
Bless those we love, and help all in need of caring.
Let my compassion shine on all around me.
May I give comfort when my loved ones need me.
Assist me in being the best friend I can be.
Help me, Lord, to be sincere in troubled times,
   and elicit the good from all things.
Lord, let me be a teacher, and teach your words and life to
   those I love and to those I encounter along life's journey.
Let my morals help those who need aid and give hope
   to bad situations.
Help my gifts of personality and love lift the spirits
   of my family and friends.

Trust helps relationships with loved ones;
   help me to tell the truth when it is difficult
   and it can greatly affect those same relationships.
Give me the power to love, Lord, and never
   to give up hope on someone who won't love.
Help me lead a life full of meaningful relationships,
   and help me be myself around those I love.
Bless those I love, both friends and family,
   but also bless those who need love and affection.
Lord, let relationships with family and friends make me
   a more complete person, and help me to keep love
   strong in my life.
In your name I pray. Amen.

KEVIN KLEINE
Loyola High School of
   Los Angeles
Los Angeles, California

LoRd, YouR LovE

Lord, your love is that as a wedding band, no beginning and no end.

Lord, you gave up your only son, Jesus Christ, to the world, this world that is full of sin and pain, this world that is supposed to be living in your image.

Lord, even though we are direct descendants of your chosen people, we do not learn from their mistakes.

Help us through the times when we do things that are not right, even though we know what the right thing is. Help us when we put people down, because when we do that we are offending you as well.

Lord, we pray that one day we as humans will walk in peace: white, black, Hispanic, and Asian.

Shine your love down upon us, Lord, and pray for us sinners.

NELSON CRUZ
Fairfield College
    Preparatory School
Fairfield, Connecticut

A Prayer Upon Waking

If it be your will, God,
Preserve me through the day.
Let my encounters be blessed,
Let my meals be blessed,
Let my comings and my goings be blessed,
And help me see your hand in all things.

BASHIR NORUDDIN
Marquette University
High School
Milwaukee, Wisconsin

Weeds aNd SeeDs

God, please dig into the roots of my heart and tear away the weeds that bind my mind to the things in life that don't matter. Dig a hole in my heart and plant seeds of your love so that I may be a better person. Water the seeds with your grace. Please allow me to continually grow and to realize that every day is a new day. Let me remember that what has happened has happened; what I do from now on is what matters. Allow me not to lose sight of that. Please guide me to the path of eternal salvation. Allow me to love with the roots of my heart, and allow these roots to grow until you come again.
Amen.

ANDREW RADACK
Strake Jesuit College Preparatory
Houston, Texas

OMniPreSeNt

The wind sweeps past in the coolness of night,
While my soul sings of the day when I will meet you.
The fierce fire and brimstone reign down deep in the earth,
And the silence of a whisper brings forth our fright.
The green grass stops very few,
But your forgiveness allows us new birth.
The fearless stars protect my sight,
And I thank you, Lord, for creating me, too.
Amen.

MARK RUTHER
St. Xavier High School
Cincinnati, Ohio

RuNNeR's PRaYeR

Lord, make me fast and agile
When I am slow and weary.

Make me strong and rested
When I am weak and tired.

Make me realize my dreams
So that I may win this race we call life.

DAVID TROTTER
Rockhurst High School
Kansas City, Missouri

PRAYER FOR PARTINGS

In some places there are circles
Of people incredibly close to each other.
Each of us is connected.
When we must separate, we
Feel sad and upset,
But others will always be with us
In mind and soul.
Amen.

BILL NIEHAUS
St. Xavier High School
Cincinnati, Ohio

PRAYER TO ST. IGNATIUS

St. Ignatius,
You who helped evangelize and spread the Great Message,
Who was able to refocus your life,
In troublesome times for yourself,
On the most important being in life.
Help us follow in your footsteps,
Through the long and troubling task,
Of refocusing ourselves on the almighty one,
God, our savior.
Amen.

JONATHAN VIGLIATURO
Rockhurst High School
Kansas City, Missouri

"Is There a God?"

I often find myself asking a question.
I ask myself if there really is a God.
I don't know the exact answer, but I have an intuition.
I don't think we all came from other planets on a giant pod;
Or an asteroid containing bacteria crashed,
  and we formed from the germs.
I think something made us,
Based on itself or on his, her, its own terms.
No one can answer my question, thus,
It's safe to say that there is a creator:
The creator who made the water and the ground
  on which we walk;
The creator who watches over us and knows
  what will happen later;
The creator who is the reason why we eat and talk.
I don't know if there really is a God,
But there is definitely a creator.

YU FUKUSHIMA
St. Xavier High School
Cincinnati, Ohio

RuNNiNG oN EMpTy

When my patience runs thin, and tomorrow
  doesn't look any better,
Lord, give me strength to continue.

SEAN BRADY
Strake Jesuit College Preparatory
Houston, Texas

A Prayer for Separated Parents

Dear Lord, help me face the daily challenge of having separated parents. Help me.

Give me the strength to overcome the difficulties I have in planning visits and help me face the tough decisions I must make.

When my parents argue, ease the rage and confusion I feel.

I also pray that you help my parents through their hard times, and that one day they will become friends.

In your name I pray. Amen.

ANONYMOUS
Jesuit High School
New Orleans, Louisiana

THROUGH ALL MY DOUBTS AND UNCERTAINTIES

O God, my Father and my Creator, Lord Jesus, my savior and the source of my strength:
I pray for your blessing that I may be a channel of your grace and love.

Your presence has always been with me.
When I was a child, I did not know you, but your love gave me joy and gladness.

When, like a small boat, I ventured upon the stormy seas of growing up,
You were there, steadfast like a lighthouse, guiding me safely along the shore.

You shone your divine light into my heart. I heard your voice calling me,
But, at first, I resisted. God, you never gave up. Your grace poured into me,
Too strong and powerful for me to ignore.

So here I am Lord, a young man, a son of your creation.
Here I am, unsure of where my life is going or
   how I shall live it.
What further journeys shall I embark upon?
   With my father and my mother, you honored me.
Help me to always cherish the relationship we share.
Thank you for my great friends with whom I laugh,
   study, and play.
Even with our differences, we seek you together.
   Through all my doubts and uncertainties, you have
been by my side.
You are my friend who lifts me up when I am down, who
rejoices in my wholeness,
And who leads me along the path of Christ.
You celebrate me for the man I have grown to be.
   Give me your blessing that I may serve and love others
as much as you love me.

MATT CHEN
Georgetown Preparatory School
North Bethesda, Maryland

FOR WHOM YOU HAVE BEEN

God, our almighty Father, I thank you for
  all you have done for me,
But more importantly for who you have been to me . . .

A friend
Who has been there to support and advise me,
Through the good times and the bad times.
When no one else was there to listen,
Your ears were full open.

A parent,
Who has been there to guide and nurture me,
When I have come home happy or sad.
When the outside world has hurt me,
You have been there to love me unconditionally.

A brother,
Who is present when no one else can help,
And in whom I can store my innermost secrets.
When the world has rejected me,
You have accepted me with open arms.

A teacher,
Who is there everyday to instruct me,
In order that I may utilize all the gifts bestowed upon me.
When no one else can pave the way for me,
You clear the road and lead me into greatness.

A teammate,
Who plays and tries like I do,
so that I can attain unity with you
When the odds do not favor me,
You give me confidence to win.

God,
You have been these and many more things in my life.
Through your love and guidance,
I have the foundation to be the best person I can.
For this and many other reasons,
I devote myself to your name.

JUBRIAL NESHEIWAT
Saint Peter's Preparatory School
Jersey City, New Jersey

WiNteR NiGhT's PRaYeR

(Author's note: It doesn't have to be snowy outside to recite this prayer. The snow is an image used to represent God's grace falling on us. Imagine looking at the snow through a window in a quiet room. Don't you feel at peace when seeing the white flakes falling softly and gently?)

As I look outside on a wintry eve,
I feel in my heart what my mind can't conceive.
I see your grace, in the wondrous flakes,
The love you give, which my heart always takes.
I hear your Word in the wind outside.
I taste your holy warmth inside.
I am calm; I have no fears.
I am warm; I have no tears.
Your grace gave me a life both dear and full.
Your light gave me a soul unbreakable.
I love you God; this I want you to know,
And all your creation, the seeds you sow.
Amen.

JHUNN VELASCO
Saint Peter's Preparatory School
Jersey City, New Jersey

Asking for Mercy

Help me God, in times of joy or despair.
Help me God, whether or not I am in need of you.
Help me God, whenever I seek hope.
Help me God, wherever I stand.
Help me God, when shadows lurk near me.
Help me God, when my judgment blinds me.
Help me God, when I am injured in mind or body.
Help me God, when I trip over my own feet.
Help me God, when I cannot reach you.
Help me God, when my soul is black.
Help me God, when I am despised.
Help me God, when I am suffering.
Help me God, with all of my troubles.
Help me God, as you have helped me before.

MARK FERMILL
Saint Peter's Preparatory School
Jersey City, New Jersey

AMDG

I am supposed to do everything in life for one reason:
   the greater glory of God.
Yet I spend most of my life unconcerned with this;
I waste it on petty things.
God, please grant me clear vision,
The vision to work for the greater glory of your name.
Please help me to wake up each morning with this in mind.
Help me to clear my mind of minor details that only
   distract me from my purpose.
Keep away the indifference that fogs humankind.
Point me where your people need help
So that I may go to bed each night knowing
   the world is a better place,
And your vision has been fulfilled.

KIRK ROBERTS
Jesuit High School
Tampa, Florida

Prayer to
St. Francis Xavier

Help me become a hero—
>One who executes both spiritual and physical feats;
>One who gives himself up to be a part of
>   something greater;

>One who departs on a journey and returns changed.

Help me to emphasize the *magis*—
>One who does his best in every area;

>One who strives to be great in all aspects of his life.

Help me become a person with and for others—
>One who respects himself as well as others;

>One who performs deeds not for himself, but for others.

Help me become a leader—
>One who persuades others to do the right thing;

>One who guides others through action, not talk.

>>We pray to you for help, St. Xavier.
>>>Amen.

LUKE ROTHAN
St. Xavier High School
Cincinnati, Ohio

PeRfecT SaCriFiCe
(A reflection on Mass and the most Holy Eucharist)

Lord, we gather at your side
As your people from all nations far and wide
We come to hear the word of God
And to join his precious body and blood

You are Jesus Christ
You died for us, you gave your life
You are Jesus Christ
You made the perfect sacrifice

Lord, we come with empty hearts
Pour your love into our lives' most empty parts
Wash us clean and make us whole
Father, send your mercy, save our souls

You are Jesus Christ
You died for us, you gave your life
You are Jesus Christ
You made the perfect sacrifice

BROCK HAMMON
Jesuit High School
Tampa, Florida

OUR SEARCH FOR JUSTICE

Lord, help our nation and its people to promote a
social policy in which society is bettered as a whole
and not merely the individual.
Help our creators of social policy to maintain an
eye for justice and not one for selfish dollar signs.
Open our nation's eyes to a world of social justice
in which one can feel safe and comfortable. One in
which heads are not looking over shoulders.
One that is fair and true in the eyes of God.
Help those communitarians who are caught up in
their theory of the betterment of the group not to
lose their compassion for the individual.
Make those individualists who can't see past
their ideals of self-improvement aware of their
selfishness and their lack of compassion for
everyone around them.
Lord, we thank you for your help throughout our
search for
social justice.
Amen.

MATT CLARK
Loyola High School of
Los Angeles
Los Angeles, California

Prayer in Time of Depression

Dear God,
I pray to you for your guidance and understanding
   at this most troublesome time.
I pray to you for your help in this most trying time of my life.
Help me to overcome this sadness that is so heavy
   on my heart and that is nearly impossible to
   overcome on my own.
Guide me away from what causes this depression
   and lead me toward what will bring happiness.
Amen.

ANONYMOUS
Jesuit High School
New Orleans, Louisiana

OUR HEADS ABOVE WATER

O, mysterious one,

In this reflection I give to you, I pour out my heart, soul, mind, and spirit. I look at all that is around me as I walk in my normal routine, I look at your mass creation, and it amazes me. I realize that I am alive, living well and to the fullest, and "waking up" as I mature today, tomorrow, and forever as long as I live. I thank you, Lord, for your life, love, and everlasting mystery that keep our heads above the water.

Amen.

BRENDAN MARSHALL
Loyola Blakefield
Towson, Maryland

Musician's Prayer

God,

You gave us the wonderful gift of music.

Many of us enjoy creating and playing music, while more
of us enjoy listening to music and relaxing with it.

The music you have given us is a wonderful
and powerful gift.

Please, help the people of the world who misuse music.

Also help musicians who have a talent but don't realize it,
and the musicians who have talent but won't use it
for others or for you.

Through your infinite mercy and kindness, we ask that
our prayers will be answered, not according to our will,
but yours. Amen.

JOEY WAGNER
Rockhurst High School
Kansas City, Missouri

Prayer to Find God in All Things

Under a leaf, in a snowflake
In a blade of grass, in a raindrop
All parts of nature

In your parents' loving embrace
In the phone call from your grandparents
All family relationships

In working and sharing with others
In helping the unfortunate
All volunteering jobs

Where are you able to find God?

Lord, help me to find you in all ways and walks of life.
Amen.

JARED KILEY
St. Xavier High School
Cincinnati, Ohio

GoD iN tHe SToRm

A storm occurred today. The sky blackened, the rain
pounded, and the wind was treacherous. Nature seemed
vicious and violent. Then the storm ended. The sky was
blue and calm. Everything was peaceful and tranquil.
The birds began to sing again. This wonderful work of
yours, Lord, has helped me realize that although my life
may become dark and cloudy, you will be there to help me,
and my life will become clear and tranquil again.

SHANE STEPHENSON
St. Xavier High School
Cincinnati, Ohio

The Pressure Prayer

Lord, why are there all these pressures in the world?
Pressure to be cool,
>To be popular,
>To be athletic,
>To be smart.

How can I be myself?

Why are there all these pressures in the world?
Pressure to decide what to be,
>What to do,
>Where to go to school,
>With whom to hang out.

How can I do what you and I want to do?
Why do I listen to these pressures?

Father, teach me to trust you, and help me to follow your will.
Give me the strength and courage to fight these pressures
  and not let them beat me down.
Lord, help me find my direction, my calling,
  my role in this world full of so many pressures.

JIM FEIN
Jesuit High School
New Orleans, Louisiana

Love of Neighbor

Dear God,
There is a special place in my heart for those
    who are less fortunate.
I feel that they need love and support just as everyone does.
Help me to be like a savior to others, as you were to us.
Helping people is what brings flavor to our lives.
The feeling of knowing that you had an impact on
    someone's life is phenomenal.
I look to you, God, for the strength and courage to do all I can
In order to help those who need me and my service,
For if I was ever in their position, I would want the same.

Thank you for the strengths and talents
    that you have given to me.
I will use them to the best of my ability
    and follow your example
To be a helping and caring person.
Amen

BILLY RABBIT
Saint Peter's Preparatory School
Jersey City, New Jersey

The World Doesn't Revolve Around Me

Dear Lord,
Help me to recognize the reasons for decisions that are made by other people. Even if I do not agree with the reasons, let me carry out the wishes that others have. Help me to recognize that not everything revolves around me, and that others need my help as much as I need their help. Help me to deal with the everyday things that make me upset. Others have the same problems, and they need help, too. Help me to learn the importance of patience. I am not the only person who needs your help.
Amen.

DENNY PERRY
St. Xavier High School
Cincinnati, Ohio

WORRIED ABOUT MOM

Dear God,

It has been a difficult time for me once again. I am very worried about my mom. She has been very silent about her health. She kept saying she didn't feel well and was very tired all the time. I know my brothers and I keep her busy, but she has not been her usual self. Please keep her in your prayers because I think she is really sick and not telling us. As it turns out, my mom told us she has a problem with her thyroid. The doctor put her on medication that should make her feel better soon. Please keep her in your prayers because if anything happens to her, I don't know where my brothers and I will end up. My brothers and I depend on her for just about everything. I understand more and more what my mother means when she says if you don't have your health, you don't have anything. Thank you, God, for all that I have.
Amen.

BRIAN STEVENSON
Saint Peter's Preparatory School
Jersey City, New Jersey

A PRaYeR BeFoRe a SeRviCe PRojecT

Dear God, those less fortunate than me need my help.
You have blessed me with so much.
Help me work in your name for those who need both
    Your help and my help.
Guide my hands and my heart so that I am capable of
    Doing your divine will.
Amen.

JACK RICHARDS
Jesuit High School
New Orleans, Louisiana

PRAYER DURING TIMES OF SICKNESS

For the first time I am learning how to deal with
   the severe sickness of a close family member.
I don't know why God's world includes these diseases
   that cannot be healed, but they are one of many
   hardships we face that nobody has discovered
   how to overcome.
I am trying to find the courage to understand that God
   knows best, but it's hard when losing a loved grandfather.
Geedaddy is the best grandfather a kid could ever have,
   and I am very fortunate to have been able
   to tell him that.
I ask God to be with my grandfather as cancer tears
   through his body, and I ask God to look over the scientist
   who is so close to discovering a cure.
It would be refreshing to know that others do not have
   to go through the same thing my family and I
   have endured.
Thank you, God, for the many years you blessed me
   with a loving and caring grandfather.

KEITH THOMPSON
Jesuit High School
Tampa, Florida

PRaYeR foR AnGrY SoNs

Dear Lord,
Help me in life when I become irritated with my parents.
Help me to understand why they do the things they do.
Let me understand that they love me and that
 They try to do everything for my betterment.
Let me have patience in dealing with them
 And help me control my anger when talking to them.
I ask this in your name. Amen.

MICHAEL SILVA
Jesuit High School
New Orleans, Louisiana

PaRenTs

When I argue with my parents, God,
Please help me to remember who they are.
I should respect them at all times
And realize that they have given me so much.
I am who I am because of how they raised me.
Help me to see myself in their position
And to understand how much parents love their kids.
I will be in their shoes someday,
And I know that parenthood is not any easy job.
They are learning as much as I am
Because this is still new to them, too.

DAN HOPMANN
St. Louis University
  High School
St. Louis, Missouri

THe BLueS

Lord, help to brighten my day.
Make my skies blue.
Put a smile on my face.
Today I have the blues.
It's another one of those days,
A horrible, no-good day.
Please, Lord, help me get through this tough day
And all the others to come.
Amen.

ADAM MOCCIOLA
Fairfield College
  Preparatory School
Fairfield, Connecticut

TRanSiTioNs

We become comfortable with our life,
Failing to challenge ourselves or be challenged by others.
It is in transitioning that we are faced with
Our biggest tribulations and most trying times.
As we continue our journey in faith, Lord,
Do not let us become overly comfortable
With the position of our faith life.
Let us be knowledgeable of our faith so that
   when we are challenged,
We can defend ourselves in your name.

DENNIS BURKE
St. Louis University
   High School
St. Louis, Missouri

THe CoMpeTitoR's PRaYeR

Lord, grant me the strength to give every ounce of energy
to my cause.
Keep everyone safe from harm or injury.
Help me on my way to greatness.
Allow me the humbleness to respect those who
perform better,
Not to tear them down.
Do not allow me to walk away
Without being completely satisfied with my effort.
Help me to compete with a demeanor
That is both representative of me and your word.
Bless my effort and help make it one of which I can be proud.
In your name I play and pray,
Amen.

RYAN WALKER
Jesuit High School
Tampa, Florida

MaRbLes

It is odd that,
To he who plays
Marbles with planets,
We are so small,
Yet so important.

CHRIS WAIT
St. Xavier High School
Cincinnati, Ohio

WHICH WAY

Up and down,
Down and up:
One day was beautiful, fun, and
Happy;
The next was dark, mean, and
Hateful.
Left? Right?
Which way was I to go?
Where were you when I was up and
Where were you when I was down?
I was alone with no one to turn to.
I searched for you,
But you were nowhere.
Today I still cannot find you.
When will you return?

COLLEEN DUGAN
Loyola Academy
Wilmette, Illinois

September 11, 2001

("God Bless America" in Context of a Catastrophe)

God, our kind Father,
God, our dear Mama,
Please bless America,
And we'll kill Osama.
But isn't this a paradox?
Is anyone aware?
Is our logic being blinded
By this horrific scare?
Maybe it's not for vengeance
If we are indeed the "big bro"
Trying to discipline our "family."
Yet our family is the foe.
But if we are brothers,
Then at most we are twins
With equal strengths of culture
And equal strengths of whims.

Many times in the description
Of our own beloved nation
We think of our great diversity
And exclaim with proud elation
That this diversity came
From our will to fight
For liberty and justice
And every U.S. right.
But can't such a blessing
From our country stem:
From a "God bless us"
To a "God bless them"?

These terrorists shocked the world.
Maybe we should, too.
Amen.

KEVIN QUINN WALSH
St. Xavier High School
Cincinnati, Ohio

PRAYER FOR THOSE WHO HAVE LOVED AND LOST

To love a woman in truth, in heart, in soul
It is a high unexplainable by any
It is a feeling of greatness
A pleasure that is stolen

Betrayal of the closest kind
Felt in the moment and instant only
The instant as his heart drops
It falls down through lead and steel
Locked in place, broken

Never will love fill it again
For fear engulfs its once joyous passion

Dear God, let those who have lost love
Fill the emptiness inside
Let them grow out of their grief
Into a better loving person with more respect for love and life

PAUL BEATTY
Jesuit High School
Tampa, Florida

New Creation

God, reshape me;
God, renew me;
God, mold me with your hands.

Forever I want to be
   In your power,
   In the light of your love.

God, reshape me;
God, renew me;
God remake my whole life.

God, refill me,
Give me joy again.
Give me peace.
Give me love.

I sometimes forget your blessings.
So now I thank you. Thank you, God.

MARK ULICSNI
Jesuit High School
New Orleans, Louisiana

THe BLeSSinG oF a YoUnG GRadUaTinG ADuLt

May God bless you as you begin your journey to the
adult world, as your high school years end.

May God bless you with the courage to face the world on
your own for the first time, to help you meet new people.

May God bless you and protect you from injury and
fear as you journey through life.

May God bless you and give you the concentration
you need to study and achieve your academic goals.

May God bless you and give you confidence to achieve
your goals as a successful businessman or businesswoman.

May God bless you and make all your hopes and
dreams come true.
Put your faith in our almighty God.
Amen.

KENNY SANTUCCI
Saint Peter's Preparatory School
Jersey City, New Jersey

Jesus: Return to the Question

One day when Jesus was praying in seclusion and his disciples were with him, he put the question to them, "Who do the crowds say that I am?"

"John the Baptizer," they replied, "and some say Elijah, while others claim that one of the prophets of old has returned from the dead." "But you—who do you say that I am?" he asked them.

Peter said in reply, "The Messiah of God."

He strictly forbade them to tell this to anyone. "The Son of Man," he said, "must first endure many sufferings, be rejected by the elders, the high priests and the scribes, and be put to death, and then be raised up on the third day."

Who do you say that I am?

It is the question that confronts us all. It demands an answer. Yet, it is a question that takes a lifetime to fully understand and answer. It is one, though, that must forever be in our thoughts and actions: "Who do you say that I am?"

Jesus is standing before me.

Not the calm babe with a halo in a stable. Not the man dying for our sins. *Jesus.*

And he stands there.

And he smiles.

And he asks me a question.

"Who do you say I am?"

I try to speak, but I cannot. The question seems so harmless, so simple. Beneath it lie years of blood and confusion and hope and pain. Beneath it lie millions of people praying for salvation, praying for something. And beneath it lies me . . . buried somewhere. He smiles again, and this time the smile asks the question.

"Who do you say I am?"

A great man. A very great man. You had a belief. You had a new way of thinking, a new way of *feeling.* In a time of betrayal and orthodoxy, you brought caring and hope. You led. You spoke. You died. It doesn't take a resurrection to make that a miracle. You, for better or worse, *changed things.* Your life changed things. Your death changed even more. You gave yourself up. You could have run. You could have fought; but you didn't want to betray yourself. You were Jewish; you probably could recite the story of David fighting Goliath by heart. The armor didn't fit him. It didn't fit you, either. You died for your beliefs. You never gave up. You are a great man.

Again. The question isn't wholly answered yet. "Who do you say I am?"

A misunderstood man. How many people were killed in your name? How many continue to abuse and hate in the name of God? For how many who were accused of being a "witch" or a "heretic" would you have gladly offered your life? Every last one. But still the hatred continues in your name. I wonder oftentimes what you would have thought. I read about an organization raising $6 million to advertise a "cure" for homosexuality—in your name. Then I wonder what *you* would have done with $6 million dollars. How many children would that feed? How many lives would that save? Then I cry.

You're still not satisfied.

The serene look in your eyes, the warm smile on your lips.

"Who do you say I am?"

I stand up, and step toward you. You make no movement; you do not avoid me. We look eye to eye, damned soul to holy Savior. I see myself reflected in your eyes; you see me, too. I stare. I wonder. I touch. I place my hand on your cheek, run my fingers over you nose. I press gently against your eyelids, as you smile again and shut your eyes. You whisper, "Who do you say I am?"

A human being. That's what you are. That's who you are. You're a man. You're a person, like me. You're not some lofty figure in heaven. You're not a prince passing eternal judgment. You're a man. You want. You laugh. You cry. You smile and breathe and walk. You bleed. And then I look at your wrists.

Drip. Drip. Drip.

You're dying. You've been dying this whole time I've looked at you, answered your enigmatic question. You stood here and bled . . .

Drip.

so I could answer your question. So I could touch your face. So I could know who you are. You didn't die on a cross. You're dying right here in front of me. The puddle on the floor . . .

Drip.

is large and black. I look at you again, and you still smile.
Only this time, a tear rolls down your cheek . . .

Drip.

and sends ripples through the blood on the floor. . . .

"Who do you say I am?"

ANDREW KERSTEN
St. Xavier High School
Cincinnati, Ohio

IGnaTiaN DaiLy EXaMinaTioN (EXaMen)

If there is one word that characterizes Ignatian spirituality, it is *discernment*—the process of looking closely at one's life and naming what is of God and what is not of God. The daily examination served Ignatius and his companions well (and all of us today who follow in his footsteps) when facing both ordinary and extraordinary decisions in their lives and ministries.

The following examen was written by Rev. Dennis Hamm, S.J., and appears in "Rummaging for God: Praying Backward through Your Day," which appeared in *America.*

A METHOD: FIVE STEPS

1. **Pray for light.** Since we are not simply daydreaming or reminiscing but rather looking for some sense of how the Spirit of God is leading us, it only makes sense to pray for some illumination. The goal is not simply memory but graced understanding. That's a gift from God devoutly to be begged. "Lord, help me understand this blooming, buzzing confusion."

2. **Review the day in thanksgiving.** Note how different this is from looking immediately for your sins. Nobody likes to poke around in the memory bank to uncover smallness, weakness, lack of generosity. But everybody likes beautiful gifts, and that is precisely what the past twenty-four hours contain—gifts of existence, work, relationships, food, challenges. Gratitude is the

foundation of our whole relationship with God. So use whatever cues help you to walk through the day from the moment of awakening—even the dreams you recall upon awakening. Walk through the past twenty-four hours, from hour to hour, from place to place, task to task, person to person, thanking the Lord for every gift you encounter.

3. **Review the feelings that surface in the replay of the day.** Our feelings, positive and negative, the painful and the pleasing, are clear signals of where the action was during the day. Simply pay attention to any and all of those feelings as they surface, the whole range: delight, boredom, fear, anticipation, resentment, anger, peace, contentment, impatience, desire, hope, regret, shame, uncertainty, compassion, disgust, gratitude, pride, rage, doubt, confidence, admiration, shyness—whatever was there. Some of us may be hesitant to focus on feelings in this over-psychologized age, but I believe that these feelings are the liveliest index to what is happening in our lives. This leads us to the fourth moment:

4. **Choose one of those feelings (positive or negative) and pray from it.** That is, choose the remembered feeling that most caught your attention. The feeling is a sign that something important was going on. Now simply express spontaneously the prayer that surfaces as you attend to the source of the feeling—praise, petition, contrition, cry for help or healing, whatever.

5. **Look toward tomorrow.** Using your appointment calendar if that helps, face your immediate future. What feelings surface as you look at the tasks, meetings and appointments that face you? Fear? Delighted anticipation? Self-doubt? Temptation to procrastinate? Zestful planning? Regret? Weakness? Whatever it is, turn it into prayer—for help, for healing, whatever comes spontaneously. To round off the examen, say the Lord's Prayer.

A mnemonic for recalling the five points: LT3F (light, thanks, feelings, focus, future).

DO IT.

Take a few minutes to pray through the past twenty-four hours, and toward the next twenty-four hours, with that five-point format.

EPILOGUE
Who Have We Become? Reflection on the Characteristics of a Graduate at Graduation

Prompt: Use the following material to help you consider your development here at school to date in the light of the five characteristics described. Take some quiet time to very honestly and thoroughly discern the progress or lack of progress you believe you have made in each area—one characteristic at a time. As you work your way through each characteristic, commit yourself to certain, clear-cut action steps which you will take to continue (or maybe begin) your growth in each of these areas.

To guide every facet of student development at Jesuit schools, their faculties have produced this summary statement of the characteristics that the graduate will have moved toward acquiring during his time at the school. Every course and every activity must work together toward fashioning a graduate who is:

Open to Growth: The ideal student at the time of graduation has matured emotionally, intellectually, physically, socially, and religiously to a level that reflects some intentional responsibility for his or her own growth and actions (as opposed to a passive, drifting, laissez-faire attitude about growth). The graduate is at least beginning to reach out in his development, seeking opportunities to broaden his/her mind, academic skills, imagination, feelings, religious awareness, and social consciousness.

Intellectually Competent: By graduation the student should exhibit a mastery of those academic requirements for advanced forms of education. While these requirements are broken down into departmental subject matter areas, the student will have developed many intellectual skills and understandings, which cut across and go beyond the academic requirements for college entrance.

Religious: The graduate should have a basic knowledge of the major doctrines and practices of the Catholic Church. The graduate also will have examined his/her own religious feelings and beliefs with a view to choosing a fundamental orientation toward God and establishing a relationship with a religious tradition and/or community. What is said here, respectful of conscience and religious background of the individual, applies to both the Catholic and non-Catholic graduate.

Loving: By graduation the student should be well on the way to establishing his/her own identity. The graduate is also on the threshold of being able to move beyond self-interest or self-centeredness in significant relationships with others. He should be able to risk some deeper levels of relationship in which one can disclose self and accept the mystery of another person and cherish the person. Nonetheless, the graduate's attempts at loving, while clearly beyond childhood, may not yet reflect the confidence and freedom of a mature person.

Committed to Doing Justice: The graduate should have achieved considerable knowledge of the many needs of local and wider communities and should be preparing for the day when he will take a place in these communities as a competent, concerned, and responsible member. The graduate should have begun to acquire the skills and motivation necessary to live as a man or woman for and with others.

PRAYERS TO BUILD FROM:
TRADITIONAL PRAYERS

The Apostles' Creed

I believe in God, the Father almighty,
  creator of heaven and earth.

I believe in Jesus Christ, his only Son, our Lord.
He was conceived by the power of the Holy Spirit
  and born of the Virgin Mary.
He suffered under Pontius Pilate, was crucified, died,
  and was buried.
He descended to the dead. On the third day he rose again.
He ascended into heaven, and is seated at
  the right hand of the Father.
He will come again to judge the living and the dead.

I believe in the Holy Spirit, the holy catholic Church,
  the communion of saints, the forgiveness of sins,
  the resurrection of the body, and the life everlasting.
Amen.

THE LORD'S PRAYER

Our Father, who art in heaven,
hallowed be thy name;
thy kingdom come;
thy will be done on earth as it is in heaven.
Give us this day our daily bread;
and forgive us our trespasses
as we forgive those who trespass against us;
and lead us not into temptation,
but deliver us from evil.
Amen.

The Hail Mary

Hail, Mary, full of grace, the Lord is with you.
Blessed are you among women,
and blessed is the fruit of your womb, Jesus.
Holy Mary, Mother of God, pray for us sinners
now and at the hour of our death.
Amen.

The Doxology

Glory be to the Father, and to the Son and to the
Holy Spirit; as it was in the beginning, is now,
and will be forever. Amen.

AN ACT OF CONTRITION

My God, I am heartily sorry for having offended you,
  and I detest all my sins because of your just punishments,
  but most of all because they have offended you, my God,
  who are all-good and deserving of all my love.
I firmly resolve, with the help of your grace, to sin no more
  and to avoid the near occasions of sin.
Amen.

THe MeMoRarE

Remember, most loving Virgin Mary, never was it heard
that anyone who turned to you for help was left unaided.
Inspired by this confidence, though burdened by my sins,
    I run to your protection for you are my mother.
Mother of the Word of God, do not despise my words of
    pleading but be merciful and hear my prayer.
Amen.

THe SeReniTy PRaYeR

God, grant me the serenity to accept
  the things I cannot change,
Courage to change the things I can,
  and Wisdom to know the difference.

Morning Offering

My God, I offer you my prayers, works, joys, and suffering
of this day in union with the holy sacrifice of Mass
throughout the world. I offer them for all the intentions of
your Son's Sacred Heart, for the salvation of souls,
reparation for sin, and the reunion of Christians. Amen

Prayer to the Holy Spirit

Come, Holy Spirit, fill the hearts of your faithful.
And kindle in them the fire of your love.
Send forth your Spirit and they shall be created.
And you will renew the face of the earth.
Let us pray.
Lord,
by the light of the Holy Spirit
you have taught the hearts of your faithful.
In the same Spirit
help us to relish what is right
and always rejoice in your consolation.
We ask this through Christ our Lord.
Amen.

Prayers from Our Ignatian Heritage: Jesuit Prayers

St. Ignatius's Prayer for Generosity

Lord, teach me to be generous.
Teach me to serve you as you deserve;
to give and not to count the cost,
to fight and not to heed the wounds,
to toil and not to seek for rest,
to labor and not to ask for reward,
save that of knowing that I do your will.

ST. IGNATIUS OF LOYOLA

PUTTING LOVE INTO PRACTICE

Love consists in sharing
what one has
and what one is
with those one loves.

Love ought to show itself in deeds
more than in words.

ST. IGNATIUS OF LOYOLA

Take, Lord, and Receive

Take, Lord, and receive all my liberty,
my memory, my understanding, and my entire will.
All I have and call my own.
Whatever I have or hold, you have given me.
I restore it all to you and surrender it wholly
to be governed by your will.
Give me only your love and grace
and I am rich enough and ask for nothing more.

ST. IGNATIUS OF LOYOLA
from the end of the
Spiritual Exercises

GOD'S GRANDEUR

The world is charged with the grandeur of God.
    It will flame out, like shining from shook foil;
    It gathers to a greatness, like the ooze of oil
Crushed. Why do men then now not reck His rod?
Generations have trod, have trod, have trod;
    And all is seared with trade; bleared, smeared with toil;
    And wears man's smudge and shares man's smell: the soil
Is bare now, nor can foot feel, being shod.

And for all this, nature is never spent;
    There lives the dearest freshness deep down things;
And though the last lights off the black West went
    Oh, morning, at the brown brink eastward, springs—
Because the Holy Ghost over the bent
    World broods with warm breast and ah! bright wings.

GERARD MANLEY HOPKINS, S.J.
English poet

The First Principle and Foundation

The goal of our life is to live with God forever.
God who loves us, gave us life.
Our own response of love allows God's life to flow into us
  without limit.

All the things in this world are gifts of God, presented to
  us so that we can know God more easily and make a
  return of love more readily.
As a result, we appreciate and use all these gifts of
  God insofar as they help us develop as loving persons.
But if any of these gifts become the center of our lives,
  they displace God
and so hinder growth toward our goal.

In everyday life, then, we must hold ourselves in balance
  before all of these created gifts insofar as we have a choice
  and are not bound by some obligation.
We should not fix our desires on health or sickness, wealth
  or poverty, success or failure, a long life or short one.
For everything has the potential of calling forth in us a
  deeper response to our life in God.

Our only desire and our one choice should be this:
I want and I choose what better leads to the
deepening of God's life in me.

ST. IGNATIUS OF LOYOLA
as paraphrased by David L. Fleming, S.J.,
from the beginning of the *Spiritual Exercises*
(guide to prayer written by Ignatius)

TEacH ME to ListeN

Teach me to listen, O God,
to those nearest me,
my family, my friends, my coworkers.
Help me to be aware that
no matter what words I hear,
the message is,
"Accept the person I am. Listen to me."

Teach me to listen, my caring God,
to those far from me—
the whisper of the hopeless,
the plea of the forgotten,
the cry of the anguished.

Teach me to listen, O God my Mother,
to myself.
Help me to be less afraid
to trust the voice inside—
in the deepest part of me.

Teach me to listen, Holy Spirit,
for your voice—
in busyness and in boredom,
in certainty and in doubt,
in noise and in silence.

Teach me, Lord, to listen. Amen.

ADAPTED BY JOHN VELTRI, S.J.

You Have Called Me By Name

Oh, Lord my God,
you called me from the sleep of nothingness
merely because in your tremendous love
you want to make good and beautiful beings.
You have called me by my name in my mother's womb.
You have given me breath and light and movement
and walked with me every moment of my existence.
I am amazed, Lord God of the universe,
that you attend to me and, more, cherish me.
Create in me the faithfulness that moves you,
and I will trust you and yearn for you all my days.
Amen.

JOSEPH TETLOW, S.J.

A Prayer for Spiritual Freedom

O Spirit of God, we ask you to help orient
all our actions by your inspirations,
carry them on by your gracious assistance,
that every prayer and work of ours
may always begin from you
and through you be happily ended.

ANONYMOUS
This prayer is frequently
used by Jesuits to begin
classes and meetings.

Wash ME with Your Precious Blood

See, O merciful God, what return
I, your thankless servant, have made
for the innumerable favors
and the wonderful love you have shown me!
What wrongs I have done, what good left undone!
Wash away, I beg you, these faults and stains
with your precious blood, most kind Redeemer,
and make up for my poverty by applying your merits.
Give me the protection I need to amend my life.
I give and surrender myself wholly to you,
and offer you all I possess,
with the prayer that you bestow your grace on me,
so that I may be able to devote and employ
all the thinking power of my mind
and the strength of my body in your holy service,
who are God blessed for ever and ever. Amen.

ST. PETER CANISIUS, S.J.

Prayer for Detachment

I beg of you, my Lord,
to remove anything which separates
me from you, and you from me.

Remove anything that makes me unworthy
of your sight, your control, your reprehension;
of your speech and conversation,
of your benevolence and love.

Cast from me every evil
that stands in the way of my seeing you,
hearing, tasting, savoring, and touching you;
fearing and being mindful of you;
knowing, trusting, loving, and possessing you;
being conscious of your presence
   and, as far as may be, enjoying you.

This is what I ask for myself
And earnestly desire from you. Amen.

BLESSED PETER FABER, S.J.
one of Ignatius's original companions

PaTieNt TRusT

Above all, trust in the slow work of God.
We are quite naturally impatient in everything
    to reach the end without delay.
We should like to skip the intermediate stages.
We are impatient of being on the way to something
    unknown, something new.
And yet it is the law of all progress
    that it is made by passing through
    some stages of instability—
    and that it may take a very long time.

And so I think it is with you;
    your ideas mature gradually—let them grow,
    let them shape themselves, without undue haste.
Don't try to force them on,
    as though you could be today what time
    (that is to say, grace and circumstances
    acting on your own good will)
    will make of you tomorrow.

Only God could say what this new spirit
    gradually forming within you will be.
Give Our Lord the benefit of believing
    that his hand is leading you,
and accept the anxiety of feeling yourself
    in suspense and incomplete.

PIERRE TEILHARD DE CHARDIN, S.J.
scientist, poet, mystic

TEACH ME YOUR WAYS

Teach me your way of looking at people:
as you glanced at Peter after his denial,
as you penetrated the heart of the rich young man
and the hearts of your disciples.

I would like to meet you as you really are,
since your image changes those with whom
    you come into contact.

Remember John the Baptist's first meeting with you?
And the centurion's feeling of unworthiness?
And the amazement of all those who saw miracles
    and other wonders?

How you impressed your disciples,
the rabble in the Garden of Olives,
Pilate and his wife,
and the centurion at the foot of the cross. . . .

I would like to hear and be impressed
by your manner of speaking,
listening, for example, to your discourse
    in the synagogue in Capharnaum
or the Sermon on the Mount where your audience
    felt you "taught as one who has authority."

PEDRO ARRUPE, S.J.
superior general of the
Society of Jesus, 1965–98

IN THE HANDS OF GOD

More than ever I find myself in the hands of God.
This is what I have wanted all my life from my youth.

But now there is a difference;
the initiative is entirely with God.

It is indeed a profound spiritual experience
to know and feel myself so totally in God's hands.

> PEDRO ARRUPE, S.J.
> superior general of the
> Society of Jesus, 1965–98

Soul of Christ (Anima Christi)

Soul of Christ, sanctify me.
Body of Christ, save me.
Blood of Christ, inebriate me.
Water from the side of Christ, wash me.
Passion of Christ, strengthen me.
O good Jesus, hear me.
Within your wounds, hide me.
Do not allow me to be separated from you.
From the malevolent enemy defend me.
In the hour of my death call me,
and bid me come to you,
that with your saints I may praise you
forever and ever. Amen

Prayers from the Ages:
Classic Prayers

Peace Prayer

Lord make me an instrument of your peace.
Where there is hatred, let me sow love.
Where there is injury, let me sow pardon.
Where there is doubt, let me sow faith.
Where there is despair, let me give hope.
Where there is darkness, let me give light.
Where there is sadness, let me give joy.
O, Divine Master, grant that I may
not try to be comforted, but to comfort;
not try to be understood, but to understand;
not try to be loved, but to love.
Because it is in giving that we receive,
in forgiving that we are forgiven,
and in dying that we are born to eternal life.

ST. FRANCIS OF ASSISI
founder of the
Franciscan Order

UNtitLed

This World is not Conclusion.
A Species stands beyond—
Invisible, as Music—
But positive, as Sound—
It beckons, and it baffles—
Philosophy—don't know—
And through a Riddle, at the last—
Sagacity, must go—
To guess it, puzzles scholars—
To gain it, Men have borne
Contempt of Generations
And Crucifixion, shown—
Faith slips—and laughs, and rallies—
Blushes, if any see—
Plucks at a twig of Evidence—
And asks a Vane, the way—
Much Gesture, from the Pulpit—
Strong Hallelujahs roll—
Narcotics cannot still the Tooth
That nibbles at the soul—

EMILY DICKINSON
American poet

HoLy SoNNeT XIV: BaTTeR My HeaRt, ThRee-PeRSoNed GoD

Batter my heart, three personed God; for you
As yet but knock, breathe, shine, and seek to mend;
That I may rise, and stand, o'erthrow me, and bend
Your force to break, blow, burn and make me new.
I, like an usurped town, to another due,
Labor to admit you, but O, to no end;
Reason, your viceroy in me, me should defend,
But is captived, and proves weak or untrue.
Yet dearly I love you, and would be loved fain,
But am betrothed unto your enemy.
Divorce me, untie or break that knot again;
Take me to you, imprison me, for I,
Except you enthral me, never shall be free,
Nor ever chaste, except you ravish me.

JOHN DONNE
English clergyman
and poet

We THaNk THee

For flowers that bloom about our feet;
For tender grass, so fresh and sweet;
For song of bird and hum of bee;
For all things fair we hear or see—
Father in Heaven, we thank Thee!

For blue of stream, for blue of sky;
For pleasant shade of branches high;
For fragrant air and cooling breeze;
For beauty of the blowing trees—
Father in Heaven, we thank Thee!

For mother-love, for father-care;
For brothers strong and sisters fair;
For love at home and school each day;
For guidance lest we go astray—
Father in Heaven, we thank Thee!

For Thy dear, everlasting arms,
That bear us o'er all ills and harms;
For blessed words of long ago,
That help us now Thy will to know—
Father in Heaven, we thank Thee!

RALPH WALDO EMERSON
American writer

Brother Sun,
Sister Moon

Most high, omnipotent, righteous Lord, to you be all
praise, glory, honour and blessing. To you alone are they
due, and no human is worthy to mention you.

Praise be to you, my Lord, for all your creatures, above all
Brother Sun, who gives us the light of day. He is beautiful
and radiant with great splendour, and so is like you most
high Lord.

Praise be to you, my Lord, for Sister Moon and the stars. In
heaven you fashioned them, clear and precious and beautiful.

Praise be to you, my Lord, for Brother Wind, and for every
kind of weather, cloudy or fair, stormy or serene, by which
you cherish all that you have made.

Praise be to you, my Lord, for Sister Water, which is useful
and humble and precious and pure.

Praise be to you, my Lord, for Brother Fire, by whom you
lighten the night, for he is beautiful and playful and robust
and strong.

Praise be to you, my Lord, for our Sister Earth, who sustains and governs us, and produces varied fruits with coloured flowers and herbs.

Praise be to you, my Lord, for those who forgive sins in your love, and for those who bear sickness and tribulation.

Blessed are those who endure in peace, for by you, most high Lord, they shall be crowned.

Praise be to you, my Lord, for our Sister Bodily Death, from whom no living person can escape. Pity those who die in mortal sin.

Blessed are those who in death are found obedient to your most holy will, for death shall do them no harm.

Praise and bless my Lord, giving him thanks and serving him with great humility.

ST. FRANCIS OF ASSISI
founder of the Franciscan Order

A Godly Meditation

Give me grace, good Lord
To count the world as nothing,
To set my mind firmly on you
And not to hang on what people say;
To be content to be alone,
Not to long for worldly company,
Little by little to throw off the world completely
And rid my mind of all its business;
Not to long to hear of any worldly things;
Gladly to be thinking of you,
Pitifully to call for your help,
To depend on your comfort,
Busily to work to love you;
To know my own worthlessness and wretchedness,
To humble and abase myself under your mighty hand,
To lament my past sins,
To suffer adversity patiently, to purge them,
Gladly to bear my purgatory here,
To be joyful for troubles;
To walk the narrow way that leads to life,
To bear the Cross with Christ,

To keep the final hour in mind,
To have always before my eyes my death,
  which is always at hand,
To make death no stranger to me,
To foresee and consider the everlasting fire of hell,
To pray for pardon before the judge comes;
To keep continually in mind the passion that Christ
  suffered for me,
For his benefits unceasingly to give him thanks;
To buy back the time that I have wasted before,
To refrain from futile chatter,
To reject idle frivolity,
To cut out unnecessary entertainments,
To count the loss of worldly possessions, friends, liberty
  and life itself as absolutely nothing, for the winning of Christ;
To consider my worst enemies my best friends,
For Joseph's brothers could never have done him as much
  good with their love and favor as they did with their
  malice and hatred.

THOMAS MORE
Lord Chancellor under King
Henry VIII

THE PILGRIM

Who would true valor see,
  Let him come hither!
One here will constant be,
  Come wind, come weather;
There's no discouragement
Shall make him once relent
His first avow'd intent
  To be a Pilgrim.

Whoso beset him round
  With dismal stories,
Do but themselves confound
  His strength the more is.
No lion can him fright;
He'll with a giant fight;
But he will have a right
  To be a Pilgrim.

Nor enemy, nor friend,
  Can daunt his spirit;
He knows he at the end
  Shall life inherit.
Then, fancies, fly away;
He'll fear not what men say;
He'll labor, night and day,
  To be a Pilgrim.

JOHN BUNYAN
author of *Pilgrim's Progress*

BReaStpLatE oF St. PaTrick

I bind to myself today the virtue of obedience of the angels, in the hope of the resurrection unto reward; in the preachings of the apostles, in the faith of confessors, in the purity of the holy virgins, in the deeds of righteous men.

I bind to myself today God's power to guide me, God's might to uphold me, God's wisdom to teach me, God's eye to watch over me, God's ear to hear me, God's word to give me speech, God's hand to guide me, God's shield to shelter me against the seductions of sin.

I invoke today all these virtues against every hostile power which may assail my body and soul, against the cries of false prophets, against the black laws of heathenism, against the deceits of idolatry, against every knowledge that binds the soul of man.

Christ, protect me today against untimely death that I may receive abundant reward. Christ with me. Christ before me. Christ behind me. Christ within me. Christ with the soldier. Christ with the traveler. Christ in the heart of everyone who thinks of me. Christ in every eye that sees me. Christ in every ear that hears me. Praise to the Lord of my salvation! Salvation in Christ the Lord.

ATTRIBUTED TO ST. PATRICK

ON MY BLinDneSS

When I consider how my light is spent,
Ere half my days, in this dark world and wide,
And that one talent which is death to hide
Lodged with me useless, though my soul more bent
To serve therewith my Maker, and present
My true account, lest He, returning, chide;
"Doth God exact day-labor, light denied?"
I fondly ask. But Patience, to prevent
That murmur, soon replies: "God doth not need
Either man's work or His own gifts: who best
Bear His mild yoke, they serve Him best. His state
Is kingly: thousands at His bidding speed,
And post o'er land and ocean without rest:
They also serve who only stand and wait."

JOHN MILTON
English poet

THE LAST INVOCATION

At the last, tenderly,
From the walls of the powerful fortress'd house,
From the clasp of the knitted locks, from the keep of the
    well-closed doors,
Let me be wafted.

Let me glide noiselessly forth;
With the key of softness unlock the locks—with a whisper,
Set ope the doors O soul.

Tenderly—be not impatient,
(Strong is your hold O mortal flesh,
Strong is your hold O love.)

WALT WHITMAN
American poet

AMAZING GRACE

Amazing grace, how sweet the sound,
That saved a wretch like me!
I once was lost, but now am found,
Was blind, but now I see.

'Twas grace that taught my heart to fear,
And grace my fears relieved;
How precious did that grace appear
The hour I first believed!

Through many dangers, toils, and snares,
I have already come;
'Tis grace hath brought me safe thus far,
And grace will lead me home.

The Lord has promised good to me,
His Word my hope secures;
He will my shield and portion be
As long as life endures.

When we've been there ten thousand years,
Bright shining as the sun,
We've no less days to sing God's praise
Than when we'd first begun.

JOHN NEWTON
slave trader turned Christian

Prayer of Oscar Romero

It helps, now and then, to step back and take a long view.
The kingdom is not only beyond our efforts,
  it is even beyond our vision.

We accomplish in our lifetime only a tiny fraction
  of the magnificent enterprise that is God's work.
Nothing we do is complete, which is another way of
  saying that the kingdom always lies beyond us.

No statement says all that could be said.
No prayer fully expresses our faith.
No confession brings perfection.
No pastoral visit brings wholeness.
No program accomplishes the church's mission.
No set of goals and objectives includes everything.

That is what we are about:
We plant the seeds that one day will grow.
We water seeds already planted, knowing
  that they hold future promise.
We lay foundations that will need further development.
We provide yeast that produces effects
  beyond our capabilities.

We cannot do everything and there is a sense of
  liberation in realizing that.
This enables us to do something, and to do it very well.
It may be incomplete, but it is a beginning, a step along
  the way, an opportunity for God's grace to enter and
  do the rest.

We may never see the end results, but that is the difference
  between the master builder and the worker.
We are workers, not master builders, ministers,
  not messiahs.
We are prophets of a future not our own.
Amen.

OSCAR ROMERO
archbishop of San Salvador

Optimists' Creed

Promise Yourself

To be so strong that nothing can disturb
your peace of mind.

To talk health, happiness, and prosperity
to every person you meet.

To make all your friends feel that there is
something worthwhile in them.

To look at the sunny side of everything
and make your optimism come true.

To think only of the best, to work only for the best
and to expect only the best.

To be just as enthusiastic about the success of others
as you are about your own.

To forget the mistakes of the past and press on to the
  greater achievements of the future.

To wear a cheerful expression at all times and
  give a smile to every living creature you meet.

To give so much time to improving yourself
  that you have no time to criticize others.

To be too large for worry, too noble for anger, too strong
  for fear, and too happy to permit the presence of trouble.

To think well of yourself and to proclaim this fact
  to the world, not in loud word, but in great deeds.

To live in the faith that the whole world is on your side,
  so long as you are true to the best that is in you.

CHRISTIAN D. LARSON

A Meditation by Cardinal Newman

God has created me
to do Him some definite service;
He has committed some work to me
which He has not committed to another.

I have my mission—
I may never know it in this life,
but I shall be told it in the next.

I am a link in a chain,
a bond of connection between persons.
He has not created me for naught.
I shall do good—I shall do His work;
I shall be an angel of peace,
a preacher of truth in my own place,
while not intending it,
if I do but keep His commandments.

Therefore I will trust Him.
Whatever I am, I can never be thrown away.
If I am in sickness, my sickness may serve Him;
in perplexity, my perplexity may serve Him;
if I am in sorrow, my sorrow may serve Him.

He does nothing in vain;
He knows what He is about.
He may take away my friends,
He may throw me among strangers,
He may make me feel desolate,
make my spirits sink,
hide my future from me—still

He knows what He is about.

CARDINAL NEWMAN
English clergyman

Please, Just Listen

When I ask you to listen to me and you start giving advice, you have not done what I asked.

When I ask you to listen to me and you begin to tell me why I shouldn't feel that way, you are trampling on my feelings.

When I ask you to listen to me and you feel you have to do something to solve my problems, you have failed me, strange as that may seem.

Listen! All I ask is that you listen, not talk or do . . . just hear me.

Advice is cheap; twenty-five cents will get you both Dear Abby and Billy Graham in the same newspaper.

And I can do for myself. I am not helpless. Maybe discouraged and faltering, but not helpless.

When you do something for me that I can and need to do
for myself, you contribute to my fear and inadequacy.

But, when you accept as a simple fact that I do feel what I
feel, no matter how irrational, then I can quit trying to
convince you and can get about the business of
understanding what's behind this irrational feeling.

And, when that's clear, the answers are obvious and I don't
need advice. Irrational feelings make sense when we
understand what's behind them.

Please listen and just hear me, and if you want to talk wait
a minute for your turn, and I'll listen to you.

RAY HOUGHTON, M.D.

The Victor

If you think you are beaten, you are.
If you think you dare not, you don't.
If you'd like to win, but think you can't,
It's almost a cinch you won't.

If you think you'll lose, you're lost.
For out in the world we find
Success begins with a fellow's will.
It's all in the state of mind.

If you think you are outclassed, you are.
You've got to think high to rise.
You've got to be sure of yourself before
You can ever win the prize.

Life's battles don't always go
To the stronger or faster man.
But sooner or later, the man who wins
Is the man who thinks he can.

C. W. LONGENECKER

AcKnowLeDGmEnTs And PeRMiSSioNS

Prayers by students of Jesuit High School, New Orleans, Louisiana, taken from *Through All the Days of Life III, The Jesuit High School Students' Prayer Book* (Third Edition), Jesuit High School, New Orleans, Lousiana. Copyright © 2000.

"Where Life Never Ends," "God's Garden," and "Bless Us" are prayers by students of Red Cloud Indian School, Pine Ridge, South Dakota, taken from *Footsteps of Wisdom,* published by and copyright © Red Cloud Indian School, Inc.

The examen written by Rev. Dennis Hamm, S.J., is an excerpt from his article "Rummaging for God: Praying backward through your day," which appeared in the May 14, 1994 *America.* Reprinted by permission.

"The First Principle and Foundation," "You Have Called Me by Name," "A Prayer for Spiritual Freedom," "Wash Me with Your Precious Blood," "Prayer for Detachment," "Teach Me Your Ways," "Patient Trust," "In the Hands of God," "Putting Love into Practice," taken from *Hearts on Fire: Praying with Jesuits,* The Institute of Jesuit Sources, St. Louis, MO, copyright ©1993. Reprinted by permission.

"Graduate at Graduation" used with permission of the Jesuit Secondary Education Association (JSEA).

"Peace Prayer" by St. Francis. *Day by Day: The Notre Dame Prayerbook for Students.* Edited by Thomas McNally, C.S.C., and William G. Storey, D.M.S. Notre Dame, Ind.: Ave Maria Press, 1975.

"Untitled" by Emily Dickinson. *Foundations of Theological Study: A Sourcebook.* Edited by Richard Viladesau and Mark Massa. Mahwah, N.J.: Paulist Press, 1991.

"Holy Sonnet XIV: Batter My Heart Three Personed God" by John Donne and "On My Blindness" by John Milton. *England in Literature, America Reads, Classic Edition,* John Pfordresher, Gladys V. Veidemanis, and Helen McDonnell. Glenview, Ill.: Scott, Foresman and Company, 1989.

"A Godly Meditation" by Thomas More and "Brother Sun, Sister Moon" by St. Francis. *The HarperCollins Book of Prayers: A Treasury of Prayers Through the Ages.* Compiled by Robert Van de Weye. New York: HarperCollins, 1993.

"We Thank Thee" by Ralph Waldo Emerson, "The Pilgrim" by John Bunyan, and "Amazing Grace" by John Newton. *The Christian's Treasury of Stories and Songs, Prayers and Poems, and Much More for Young and Old.* Edited and compiled by Lissa Roche. Wheaton, Ill.: Crossway Books, 1995.

"The Last Invocation" by Walt Whitman. *The Chief American Poets, Selected Poems by Bryant, Poe, Emerson, Longfellow, Whittier, Holmes, Lowell, Whitman and Lanier.* Edited by Curtiss Hidden Page. Boston: Houghton, Mifflin Company, 1905.

"Breastplate of St. Patrick." *Through All the Days of Life III: The Jesuit High School Students' Prayer Book (Third Edition).* Edited by Nicholas T. Schiro. New Orleans: The Jesuit High School, 2000.

"Please Just Listen" by Ray Houghton, M.D., reprinted with permission from *Teen Times,* the national magazine of Future Homemakers of America, Vol. 35, No. 2.

iNdEx oF AutHoRs aNd PRaYeR TitLes